RELIGION IN
A NEW KEY

SECOND EDITION

M. DARROL BRYANT

PUBLISHED BY
PANDORA PRESS

National Library of Canada Cataloguing in Publication Data

Bryant, Darrol M.

Religion in a New Key

2nd ed.
First ed. published as transcripts of 3 lectures to
which 3 essays have been added.

Includes bibliographical references.

ISBN 1-894710-18-5

1. Religions—Relations. I. Title.

BL410.B78 2001   291.1'72   C2001-904310-4

RELIGION IN A NEW KEY SECOND EDITION

Copyright © 2001 by Pandora Press
33 Kent Avenue
Kitchener, Ontario, N2G 3R2

International Standard Book Number: 1-894710-18-5
Printed in Canada on acid-free paper

10 09 08 07 06 05 04   10 9 8 7 6 5 4 3

Table of Contents

Preface to the Second Edition   7

Preface to the First Edition   10

PART I   Three Essays on Dialogue as a New Key in the Study of Religion

I   From the Traditional to the Modern Through to the Post-Modern Study of Religion   17

II   Dynamics of Interfaith Encounter and Dialogue   37

III Notes Towards the Symphony of Living Faiths   56

PART II Three Essays In the Dialogue of Religions

IV Inter-Religious Dialogue: The Problems and Prospects of Overcoming "History"   76

V   Engaging One Another: A Christian at Eiheiji (Japan) And Kumsan-Sa (Korea)   100

VI The Kumbha Mela: A Festival and Sacred Place   119

Preface

Second Edition

In the fall of 2000, fifteen students, mostly from the University of Waterloo, went with me to India for a Study Term Abroad. I had named the course "An Encounter with the Living Religions of India." Over three months, we travelled as far north as Dharamsala to visit the Tibet Buddhist community in exile and as far south as the Hindu temple city of Madurai. We also visited the Muslim community in New Delhi, the Sikhs and the Golden Temple in Amritsar, the Hindu Lingayat community in Bangalore and Sirigere, and the Christian community in Kerala. In Vrindaban, a pilgrimage city devoted to Krishna and Radha, we celebrated Diwale. In Karnataka in South India, we visited Bylakuppe and saw Tibet's great Sera Monastery being reborn. We learned that it now has nearly 6,000 monks. We walked up the stone hill at Sravanabelagola to see the granite image of the Jain Bahubali.

In the ashram city of Rishikesh in northern India, I wandered into a bookstore and found a copy of the first edition of *Religion in a New Key*. It then occurred to me that it was still a useful text but that I had done a great deal in the area of the dialogue of religions since 1987 — indeed, this course was part of the approach to the study of religion that I had written about in 1987.

It was only in 2001 that I was able to return to the project of revising and supplementing the earlier edition of this little volume. The original three essays have been slightly revised and, in a few places, updated. They remain as Part I of the volume. The substantial change is the addition of three new essays that deal with the themes of encounter and dialogue, themes central to the original lectures. They are found here as Part II of this volume. A few comments about the additional essays will help to establish their context and relate them to the purposes of *Religion in a New Key*.

In *Religion in a New Key*, I argue that the dialogue of men and women of different faiths provides the context for a new approach to the study of religion. The essays added here contribute to that proposal. The first explores some of the problems—as well as the promise—of the dialogue of religions. It argues that we must "overcome history" if the dialogue of people of different faiths is to realize its promise. It focuses on dialogue with Muslims, Hindus, and Christians and was first presented at the Iranian Embassy in New Delhi. The second essay deals with an encounter with Buddhists in Korea and Japan. In the mid-nineties, I was able to visit the monasteries of Kumsan-sa and Shimwon-am in Korea and Eiheiji in Japan. Here, the dialogue of religions moves beyond the exchange of ideas and moves into sharing in another's life and practice. In these settings, I was able to participate in the prayers and meditation of the Chogye Buddhists in Korea and the Soto Zen Buddhists of Japan, as well as discuss their Buddhist practice and ideas. The third essay deals with the world's largest religious event, the Kumbha Mela. The maha-Kumbha Melas, the great festivals of the pitcher/pot, occur every eleven or twelve years at the confluence of the Ganges and Yamuna rivers outside Allahabad (Prayag) in northern India and attract millions of pilgrims. In 1989, there were an estimated 15 million people, and in 2001 an estimated 20 million. I was able to attend both of these Festivals, thanks to the kind invitation of Srivatsa Goswami of Vrindaban. The essay is a report on my experience of the Kumbha Mela and my efforts to understand this remarkable event.

I trust that together, these three additions to the volume will further clarify and deepen the reader's understanding of the approach to the study of religion I outlined in the first edition of this volume.

October 30, All Saints Day, 2001

Preface

First Edition

The first three essays in this volume were first given as lectures in 1986-87 at the Indian Institute of Islamic Studies in New Delhi and the Dr. S. Radhakrishnan Institute for Advanced Studies in Philosophy at the University of Madras. I wish to thank Dr. Syed Ali, Director of the Indian Institute of Islamic Studies, and Dr. R. Balasubramaniam, Director of the Dr. S. Radhakrishnan Institute for Advanced Studies in Philosophy at the University of Madras, for their invitations to deliver these lectures. They provided me with the opportunity to reflect upon where we are in the study of religion and to sketch a possible new direction arising from the experience of dialogue between men and women of different faiths.

It is the experience of dialogue that constitutes the "new key" that is explored here. Thus it seems fitting that these lectures should have been offered in the context of my sabbatical in India. It was my presence in India that gave me the opportunity to further my own dialogue with a number of Indian colleagues and believers from different traditions. Though they are a silent presence in these lectures, they were never far from my awareness as I worked on these explorations.

In addition to Dr. Ali and Dr. Balasubramaniam and their families, I think especially of Sri Shrivatsa Goswami and his family who welcomed me and my family to Vrindaban, sharing with us the Festival of Dance devoted to Krishna and Radha and later the Festival of Diwali. He and his family gave us a glimpse of the depth of devotion that makes Vrindaban such a remarkable city of pilgrimage. Our pilgrimage around Vrindaban will be long remembered, as will our later time together in Benares. It was Shrivatsa Goswami and his family that began to open the Hindu world to me at a level beyond books and studies.

I also remember with appreciation the friendship of the Venerable Doboom Tulku who paved the way for several remarkable encounters with Tibetan Buddhists in Dharamsala, and the Director of the Institute of Buddhist Dialectics, Lobsang Gyatso, who shared with us the wisdom of his tradition and its meditation.

I am grateful to Dr. Mohinder Singh, Director of the Guru Nanak Institute, who was my guide into the Sikh world, and his family with whom we shared meals and conversation.

I learned a new face of the Christian tradition through my conversations with the Metropolitan Paulos Mar Gregorios, a Syrian Orthodox Bishop, who taught me something of Indian Christianity in those luminous days together in New Delhi and the Old Seminary in Kottayam, Kerala.

I appreciated the experience of learning about dialogue at the grassroots from Father Albert Nambiaparambil, a pioneering figure among Roman Catholics in India, at his Satsung Centre in Thodupuzda in Kerala.

I was deeply grateful for the opportunity to visit Shantivanam and to meet Dom Bede Griffiths and, later, Sister Vandana Mataji at Jeevan Dhara, and to become aware of their remarkable experiments in dialogue. Dr. Homi Dhalla and his family were extraordinarily generous to us and gave us a glimpse into the Zoroastrian world in Bombay and shared their home with us in Pune. I appreciated the opportunity for discussions with Dr. Freny Mehta, a Zoroastrian psychiatrist, at her home at Land's End. I would be remiss if I failed to mention the conversations with Dr. Meenakshi Gopinath, now

President of Lady Sri Ram College in the University of Delhi, and her husband Rajiv Meerohtra, a maker of beautiful films. Together they have have moved across boundaries that often separate the Hindu and Buddhist worlds, and I profited from their experience.

I also remember with appreciation the times with Dr. T. S. Devadoss and his family in Madras.

I was grateful for the opportunity to meet with the Venerable Samdhong Rimpoche at the Central Institute for of Higher Tibetan Studies at Sarnath and the opportunity to meditate on the grounds where Lord Buddha gave his first sermon.

I was honoured by the invitation to visit and lecture at the Indian Institute for Advanced Studies in Simla and remember with pleasure the vistas and conversations with Dr. Margaret Chatterjee, then its Director.

The warmth of Dr. Indira Rothermund and our conversations at the Centre for Development Studies and Education in Pune were also appreciated, especially the opportunity to visit some villages in the area. There I saw some of the village consequences of the conversion of "untouchables" to neo-Buddhism. To all of these people and to many others unnamed here, I want express my thanks for inviting us into your homes, your lives, your traditions, and your faiths. It was this human context that made for us the experience of dialogue in India so rich, rewarding, transforming and memorable.

A special mention must be made again of Dr. and Mrs. Syyed Ali and their daughters Lena and Muna. With them we shared meals and life, as well as conversation, almost daily for over two months. It was such a sustained privilege to come to know this remarkable family and to learn from them while we shared our daily bread. We cannot adequately say what that meant to all of us. But our stay with the Ali family was the grace note for our time in India.

These essays have been slightly revised since they were given, but I have tried to incorporate the criticisms and suggestions that arose in the conversations that followed their delivery in New Delhi and Madras. The press of other events has delayed my attention to their revision, but I have been encouraged by others who have read them, especially my colleague and friend Dr. Stanley Johannesen, to proceed with their publication in this largely unaltered state. Something of the immediate context in which they were written and delivered still comes through, and I believe that is appropriate. For, as I argue in these essays, we need strive not so much for an empty neutrality in the study of religion as for a shared insight and process that can be acknowledged across tradition and culture. It is my hope that these essays meet that standard and can be a slight token of the gratitude that I continue to feel towards my colleagues and friends in India. They taught me that the living dialogue emerging in our time is a suitable and vibrant key not only for living our respective faiths and lives, but also for the study of the religious heritage of humankind.

Easter Week, 1990
Elmira, Ontario, Canada

13

PART I

Three Essays on Dialogue as a New Key in the Study of Religion

Jesus of the Living Water, Jevan Dhara Ashram,
Jaiharikal, Himalayas

I
From the Traditional to the Modern
Through to the Post-Modern Study of Religion

In this essay I would like to share with you some of my reflections on where we are in the study of religion. The central thesis that lies at the heart of these reflections is this: the encounter between men and women of the great religious traditions, whether in the centres of learning, the crossroads of cities, the byways of villages, or the inwardness of human hearts, requires a reorientation in the study of religion. That reorientation will build on the real achievements of the past centuries of scholarship but also introduces a new dimension arising from our awareness of being part of an emerging planetary consciousness. In that emerging planetary consciousness — perhaps best symbolized by the image of our blue planet hurtling through space against the backdrop of infinite mystery — we will have to come to understand ourselves anew. And in that renewed understanding, we will come to see the religious pathways of humankind as diverse but interpenetrating ways into the mystery which we all share as the very context of our being — what we are and what we are becoming.

This note has been sounded in the Indian context by rishis and sages throughout the centuries. But, more recently, an analogous point has been made by Dr. Radhakrishnan in his volume on *Religion and Culture*. Here he remarks:

if there is any phenomenon which is characteristic of our times, it is the mingling of peoples, races, cultures and religions. Never before has such a meeting taken place in the history of our world.[1]

But no one, to my knowledge, has sought to develop the implications of this fact for the study of religion as we are attempting to do here.

The very fact of my being invited to give these lectures is evidence of the new and transforming situation in which we find ourselves. It is also evidence that the modern study of religion has given rise to an international community of scholarship that makes it possible for me, a Christian from the United States teaching in a Canadian university, to be here in this distinguished Indian Institute of Islamic Studies to speak about the contemporary study of religion. As a young boy growing up on the plains of North Dakota under a boundless sky alive with dancing clouds, I certainly never dreamed that I would someday be walking, together with my family, on the sun drenched soil of India attempting to hear and sense the rhythms and patterns of being that have emerged in lives of Indian Muslims who have heeded the call of Allah, or the lives of Hindus in Vrindaban who have heard the flute of Krishna, or the lives of Buddhists who strive along the "middle way" in search of "enlightenment," or the lives of Sikhs who have heeded the songs of Guru Nanak. But here I am and here we are—all of us together—caught up in a great transformation that is our common future.

As a way into our topic I want to begin by reviewing certain developments and trends in the study of religion. In this review I make no pretense of offering a sketch of the whole field nor of narrating all the trends discernible in the study of religion. Rather, my attention will focus on those figures, works, and issues that I consider most fruitful for the future of the study of religion, a future oriented to the living encounter of persons from the different religious traditions. To understand why I have given prominence to this living encounter, it is necessary to review, briefly and schematically, the history of the study of religion as it emerged in the West.

The Emergence of the Modern Study of Religion

It is important to remind ourselves that the modern study of religion is comparatively recent and is to be distinguished from traditional religious scholarship. In traditional religious scholarship, the task of the scholar was explicating the content of a given religious tradition by immersing himself in the sacred literature of the tradition. The scholar was expected to be — and was — a deeply believing member of the tradition that he sought to expound. Often, especially in the traditions centred around a sacred scripture, the primary task was to write commentaries on the sacred tests, or elaborations on the meaning of ritual, or expositions of the philosophical consequences of the revelation that was the touchstone of the tradition. Or the scholar might be a guru or guide on the spiritual disciplines and path of a given tradition. But in the modern study of religion, especially in the modern West, a new type of scholar emerged. This new scholar of religion was often in conflict with the traditional scholar because his scholarship rested on different premises. And those premises were often antagonistic to the religious traditions themselves.

The modern study of religion, especially in Western Europe and North America, sought to free itself from the tutelage of the Church and the premises of dogmatic Christianity. Although the universities of Europe had long had faculties of theology, it was only towards the end of the nineteenth century that they begin to establish chairs in the field of the history of religion and the comparative study of religion. When studies of non-Christian religions occurred in the context of the older faculties of theology, they were largely for apologetic purposes — that is, in order to show the weaknesses of other traditions and the superiority of Christianity. In contrast, the modern disciplines of comparative religion sought to place the study of religion on a new footing. That new footing was to be neutral, i.e., not biased towards any religion. What thus emerged was an approach to the study of religion that was a) historical, b) descriptive, and c) analytic. In this approach to religion it was not necessary for one to be a believer, indeed that was often seen as a hindrance because, it was argued, that qualified one's neutrality.

In North America a similar pattern is discernible: the modern study of religion emerges out of a prolonged conflict with Christian theology. Consider, for example, Harvard University, a school founded by the Puritans in 1635 for the training of a "learned ministry." Despite its long tradition of learning—and, for example, the classic studies by William James in the *Varieties of Religious Experience*, actually given as the Gifford Lectures in Scotland, and Josiah Royce at the turn of the century—it was only in the 1970s that Harvard College introduced a program of religious studies under Wilfred Cantwell Smith, a Canadian and a distinguished scholar of Islam, as its first director. And more generally in both the United States and Canada, it was only after the Second World War, and especially in the 1950s and 1960s, that departments of religious studies were established.[2] These departments were to be devoted to the academic study of religion, a study to be rigorously distinguished from the teaching of religion. (Here, one may teach about religion but not religion as such because that is proselytizing).

In this history are to be found certain gains. Most important is the concern for a fair, objective, and descriptive account of the different religious traditions as well as a freeing of the study of religion from the constraints of Christian apologetics. But this history has a darker side as well, a side that must be overcome if we are to achieve the true promise of the study of religion.

Beyond the Modern Study of Religion

Concerning the study of religion at its best, we might agree with Ninian Smart's conviction that

> The history of religions is delicate and has a sensitive soul; and as such it represents a great achievement — a distancing, and yet a warmth; objectivity and yet subjectivity of spirit; description but also evocation; method but also imagination. It is one aspect of the nobility of the best of the humanities and social sciences — a nobility which expresses itself in a willingness to enter into the experiences of others . . . .[3]

But this is, in fact, a post-modern description, because it is precisely the reluctance to enter into the experience of others and to take that experience seriously on its own grounds that characterizes the modern study of religion.

This is the darker side of the modern study of religion, one that emerges from the modern form of culture in which it emerged. That darker side has both a material and formal aspect. First, the material aspect. In the very process of freeing itself from the tutelage of the Church and the restrictions of dogmatic Christianity, the modern study of religion drank deeply at the wells of the Enlightenment, especially an Enlightenment that said a resounding "NO" to religion while enshrining technical reason (in science and elsewhere) as the engine for the creation of a specifically modern world, a brave new world. In that Enlightenment mentality — a mentality that curiously shares something with the longer history of Christianity, and especially Protestantism, in the West — is the view articulated by Voltaire that "religion is superstition," or at best, as Comte later said, a primitive state of consciousness that we will soon outgrow. Later a second great son of the Enlightenment, Karl Marx, would argue that religion was "the opiate of the people" — a way of masking the terrible injustice rooted in the means of production by promises of a heaven in which all would be resolved. And still later, a third

21

great offspring of the Enlightenment, Sigmund Freud, would argue that "religion is an illusion." To be sure, this was better than calling it a delusion, since illusions are usually benign, even though they reflect an immature response to the terrors of coming face-to-face with reality. This darker side of the modern project has bequeathed to the study of religion a stubborn reductionism that continually attempts to transform religion into something else, to reduce it to an epiphenomenon of philosophy, economics, or psychology.[4]

While each of these Enlightenment critiques of religion had their grain of truth, they also tended to undercut our seeing the reality lived and experienced by the great religious traditions of humankind. Whether encountered in the Divine Imperatives of Allah, or the Divine Insights of the Upanishads, or the Divine Emptiness of Buddha, the great religious traditions opened onto a view of human existence that was quite other than that found in those Enlightenment views, which reduced the whole of reality to what could be known through the reductionist methods of modern science or by the methods of the modern study of religion. All religion is rooted in a Beyond, an Ultimate, a Transcendent that cannot be contained within the ideological and methodological constraints of the modern study of religion.

Thus the formal aspect of the dark side of the modern study of religion is its rejection of the theological and metaphysical foundations of the phenomena of religion. This lack of an adequate metaphysical foundation has far too often left the study of religion subject to whatever ideological currents are fashionable within the academy. And in the modern world those have been the ideologies of relativism, secularism, historicism, and technical rationalism. While each of these needs to be carefully analyzed and explained, I will have to be content with two brief observations. First, these ideologies result from the rejection of metaphysics and ontology as the way into an account of the very nature of things. And secondly, they are united in their rejection of anything real beyond what can be conceived in terms of a two dimensional logic or a two dimensional reality. These ideologies have resulted in a levelling of reality to what is materially tangible.

A similar point was made by Prof. Seyyed Hossein Nasr, the well-known scholar of Sufism currently teaching in the United States, when he remarked that

> The study of religions . . . has been coloured by the mentality of modern Western man and seen under categories which have been either borrowed from later developments of Christianity or from reactions against Christianity. But in any case that metaphysical background which is indispensable for a study in depth of religion has generally been lacking.[5]

This heritage of antagonism towards religion that comes out of the Enlightenment coupled with the resulting ideologies that reject the Beyond as constituting what is in the order of space and time, have, in my view, seriously crippled the modern study of religion. It is only as these aspects of the modern study of religion are overcome that we can get on with the real tasks of the study of religion, namely, in the words of Professor Nasr, "to gain knowledge of other traditions and accept them as spiritually valid ways and roads to God."[6]

I have dealt with these trends in the study of religion at such length because I believe that the modern study of religion tends to lead us away from religion, whereas the post-modern (a study that begins with a hermenuetic of wonder rather than one of suspicion) will lead us into its depths.

The post-modern study of religion, then, will be characterized by a deep and abiding love for religion itself as the human forms of the Divine made known in the course of human history. It will not seek to reduce religion to something else, but it will seek to understand it in its own varied terms. It will not impose on religion methods foreign to its own presuppositions but seek to let those methods arise from the universal and varied forms of religious life and expression themselves. Its concern will not be to explain away religion, but to understand what has been given to us in the varied patterns of religious life through the ages.

Pioneers in the "Post-Modern" Study of Religion

Within the modern era in the West, we have seen already the emergence of movements that have sought to overcome the debilitating consequences of modernism understood as the reductionist mentality outlined above. Some efforts to move beyond reductionism are evidenced in phenomenology as it emerged in the study of religion and sought to penetrate into the structures and dynamics of religion itself. In part this corrective in the study of religion was due to a faithful adherence by the phenomenologist to the actuality of religious life which was always predicated on the experience of a Beyond, even when that Beyond was manifest in the depths of the human spirit or soul, and even when that very difference was itself overcome in an all-embracing monism. The point is that the encounter with religion in what G. van der Leuw, the remarkable Dutch scholar, called its "essence and manifestation" required a break with the implicit metaphysical conceits of modernism.[7] How could we, in our study of religion, acknowledge the Beyond that is its animating heart? Or at least, recognize that an aspiration for the Beyond is at the centre of religious life in all its universal variety?

These developments, within the European academy especially, were nourished by increased contact with non-Western traditions and cultures that had not been so infected by what Walter Lippmann once called "the acids of modernity."[8] S. H. Nasr's comment that "often a simple peasant has a more universal conception of Islam than a university educated rationalist"[9] could be applied to other traditions as well. Through field studies of actual religious life in various parts of the world and through the efforts of some truly outstanding scholars of religion—for example, Rudolph

Otto and his *Idea of the Holy*—some new currents were beginning to emerge within the study of religion.

Rather than attempt to chronicle those developments, I want to turn my attention to a few figures in what I am now calling the "post-modern" study of religion.

Mircea Eliade and the Recovery of the Integrity of Religion

One of the most important figures in the study of religion in North America was Mircea Eliade. Born in Romania in 1907, he was educated in Bucharest and in India. He came to the United States in the late 1950s and taught at the University of Chicago until his death. Over an exceptionally productive lifetime he wrote a number of studies that are already classics in the field. His little volume *The Sacred and the Profane* is still the best introduction to the nature of religion that I know.[10] A gifted student of languages, Professor Eliade read widely, bringing the contributions of many into a coherent and impressive synthesis. He has done much to establish the "History of Religions" as a respected discipline within the university.

In this context, however, I wish to focus our attention on his contribution to the recovery of the integrity of religion as "a way of being in the world." Let me quote Eliade from the preface to his multi-volumed magnum opus, *A History of Religious Ideas*, a work that remains unfinished due to his death. Here, Eliade writes:

> For the historian of religions, every manifestation of the sacred is important: every rite, every myth, every belief or divine figure reflects the experience of the sacred and hence implies the notions of being, of meaning, and of truth. As I observed on another occasion, 'it is difficult to imagine how the human mind could function without the conviction that there is something irreducibly real in the world; and it is impossible to imagine how consciousness could appear without conferring a meaning on a man's impulses and experiences. Consciousness of

a real and meaningful world is intimately connected with the discovery of the sacred. Through experiences of the sacred, the human mind has perceived the difference between what reveals itself as being real, powerful, rich and meaningful and what lacks these qualities . . . .' In short, the "sacred" is an element of the structure of consciousness and not a stage in the history of consciousness. On the most archaic levels of culture, living, considered as being human, is in itself a religious act for food-getting, sexual life, and work have a sacramental value. In other words, to be—or, rather, to become—a man signified being 'religious.'[11]

Here Eliade summarizes his conviction, borne out of decades of study, that being religious lies at the heart of being human. He testifies to his dissent from modern historicism in recognizing that "the sacred" is not a stage to be overcome but constitutes the very structure of consciousness of humanity. And he makes clear his awareness that the study of religion leads us into the Real that men and women have experienced in manifold forms from the beginning of time to the present. Eliade argues that in the present, especially in the modern West, we have sought to camouflage the religious quest for being.

As a discipline within the humanities, the study of religion remains more an art than a science, and few will be able to achieve what a master such as Eliade has achieved. But he can stand for us as a fitting example of what a true scholar of religion can become. Not only was he able to restore the dignity and integrity of religion, but he was also able to lead us more deeply into the complex symbolism of religious life and experience. Eliade took to heart the remark of Bede Kristensen, the Scandinavian scholar of religion, that "the believer is always right," and he taught a whole generation of scholars how to unravel the complexities and nuances of religious symbolism. In the language of religious life, Eliade showed us, the Beyond "speaks" or "reveals itself."[12] However, this is not a utilitarian or objective language, but one that reveals "a modality of the real or a structure of the World." For example, the symbol of the Cosmic Tree "reveals the World as a living totality."[13] Thus when we learn to read religious symbols aright, we are led into

> . . . a more profound, more mysterious life than that which is known through everyday experience. They reveal the miraculous, inexplicable side of life, and at the same time the sacramental dimensions of human existence. "Deciphered" in the light of religious symbols, human life reveals a hidden side; it comes from "another part," from far off; it is "divine" in the sense that it is the work of the gods or of supernatural beings.[14]

In Eliade we have an approach to the study of religion that can overcome some of those darker aspects of the modern study of religion. It is a way that respects the phenomena of religion so profoundly that it is willing to be instructed by what they show or reveal to us. And in that very process we are lead beyond ourselves to an endlessly fascinating Mystery.

Huston Smith and the Recovery of the Ontological in Religion

A second development and trend in the study of religion surrounds the work of Huston Smith, longtime professor of philosophy at M.I.T. and retired professor emeritus from Syracuse University. Huston Smith was born into a missionary family in China where he lived until he returned to the United States to attend university. He is the author of the best selling *The World's Religions*, a splendid introduction to the several religious traditions. More recently, he has turned his attention in another, but related, direction. In 1976, he published his *Forgotten Truth, the Primordial Tradition*. Nourished in part by his contact with Frithjof Schuon, Smith seeks in this work to unfold the "primordial tradition," the basic ontology or worldview that, he argues, has been common to the history

27

of humankind "with the sole notable exception" of modern civilization. While it is not possible to explicate that primordial worldview in detail, it is possible to highlight some of its features.[15]

First, Smith notes that "the view of reality as consisting of graded levels of being dominated man's outlook until the rise of modern science."[16] Heavens/Earth/Hells or Higher Planes/Earth/Lower Planes, in which the different levels were distinguished by the quality of being were the common backdrop of human experience until our time. To be sure, this hierarchical ordering of things was articulated in diverse terms and ways, but nonetheless reveals this common structure and conviction. The point was that there were things or dimensions of being, that were higher and lower, not in the literal sense of modern materialism, but in the primordial sense of quality. We might rise to the love of god or fall to the captivity of demons. We might see into the Truth of Things or remain caught in the maya of our attachments. We might move towards Dharma or remain caught in suffering. For corresponding to the "levels of reality" found in the primordial tradition were "levels of selfhood."[17] As Smith puts it, "As without, so within—the isomorphism of man and the cosmos is a basic premise of the traditional outlook."[18]

What Smith then richly illustrates is the patterns of correspondence to be found in the literature of religion that points to this shared outlook. Corresponding to the cosmology that moves from the terrestial, to the intermediate, on to the celestial, and finally the infinite is a pneumatology or science of the spirit that recognizes in humanity the levels of body, mind, soul, and spirit. Thus what Smith elaborates is the rich ontological tradition that lies embedded in the religious history of humankind, a tradition that in its richness discloses the poverty of the worldview embedded in modern scientism, the view that would reduce reality to the space/time continuum of modern science. (A view, parenthetically, that is rejected by great scientists like Albert Einstein, who knew the limits of his perspective and recognized how science opens out onto realms of infinite beauty and mystery.) Thus there is, in Smith's view, no need for the student of religion to continually apologize to the so-called "modern man" for the subject he studies. Rather, he might enter into a critical dialogue with the modern worldview precisely for the sake of recovering something of that great primordial tradition that is, in Smith's words, an "invisible geometry" that "has everywhere been working" to shape the great traditions to "a single truth."[19]

Of course much more needs to be said about Smith's important work, but I must hasten on. In discussing these figures, I am not suggesting that we cannot quarrel with their findings or with their particular interpretations. I am rather emphasizing their importance for the study of religion, in providing approaches that we could profitably follow, since they move us beyond the limitations of the modern assumptions that hamper that study. And Huston Smith has shown us the importance of the ontology to be found in the primordial tradition.

Wilfred Cantwell Smith and the Recovery of Tradition

A third important figure in the development of what I am calling the post-modern study of religion is Wilfred Cantwell Smith, a Canadian scholar of Islam and for several years Director of Harvard's Center for World Religions. Over the past two decades, ever since the publication of his work *The Meaning and End of Religion*, Cantwell Smith has rigorously challenged the tendency to treat religions as abstractions like "Christianity," "Buddhism," etc.[20] He has rather argued for attention to the faith of persons who are Muslims, Sikhs, Hindus, Christians, Buddhists, etc. Thus we should seek to understand persons of the different faiths in order to see the world as, for example, a Buddhist sees it. But in what has been called this "personalist" approach, Smith does not devalue the role and place of larger collectivities of believers. He sim-

29

ply emphasizes that believers stand in traditions, a living process of handing over from generation to generation a living faith that is embodied in human lives. As he says, "the most important single matter to remember in all this (the study of religion) is that ultimately we have to do not with religions but with religious persons."[21] Thus Smith would direct our attention to the lives of people, communities, and traditions in that infinitely varied process of living what has been given to us from Beyond.

The implicit direction of Wilfred Cantwell Smith's approach to the study of religion is revealed in his recent book *Towards a World Theology*. Here Smith offers a "vision" of "the unity or coherence of humankind's religious history." This unity, Smith contends, is "a matter of empirical observation. It is an historical fact." Thus he breaks with the modernist assumption of discontinuity between history and theology, between fact and value, and reasserts that "the history of religion . . . is intrinsically the locus of both the mundane and the transcendent, unbifurcated."[22] While his study has generated considerable controversy, my point here concerns his attempt to move towards a new way of studying the religious life of humankind. He is not asserting "that all religions are the same," but rather that religious traditions can "be understood only in terms of each other: as strands in a still more complex whole."[23] This challenging vision will certainly have its critics, but we can see here an important new departure that has important consequences for the future of the study of religion.

Ursula King and the Recovery of Women in Religion

A fourth important development with profound implications for the study of religion is the women's movement, a development that began in the West but has now touched our entire globe. Again, we will have to review this development altogether too briefly, but it cannot be passed over in silence. It is difficult to know how to assess the current ferment and discussion of women's experience, roles, contributions, and place in the study of religion except to acknowledge that they are substantial in the history of humankind's religious life. We have all become aware that the story of the religious life of humankind has been skewed by a gender bias that has failed to give to women their proper due in that story.

Among the many voices that are currently exploring the meaning of the experience of women for the study of religion, one of the most significant voices is that of Dr. Ursula King, Head of Theology and Religious Studies at the University of Bristol in Great Britian. Like the others reviewed here, her life and background has important cross cultural components. Born in Germany, King was educated in India and France and brings to the study of the experience of women an important background in the history of religion as well as theology. Her recent study—*Women and Spirituality, Voices of Protest and Promise*—synthesizes a good deal of the current discussion and provides a reliable guide to this important area of study. In her study she makes the crucial point that in

> . . . listening to the voices of contemporary women, we must first of all investigate the feminist challenge to traditional religion. We must also listen to women's claims about the nature and power of their own experience as well as about those experiences from which they strive to be liberated.[24]

What is especially important here is the methodological observation that we must learn to listen, to take seriously and on their own terms the voices of that gender that has been too often ignored in the study of religion. It is not an issue of assenting to this or that interpretation but of learning to hear the voice of those who have been excluded. This point is especially important in the context of the current dialogue between men and women of different faiths, for an important aspect of that dialogue is the experience of women articulating their experience and men learning to listen to that experience in its own terms and then moving to a level of mutuality.

31

Professor King makes an additional point that is especially important in this context. She rejects a view of the women's movement which would see it in only secular terms. One of the contributions King has made to the women's movement is her interpretation of the spirituality that is inherent within the women's movement itself. And thus King makes the crucial point that "the protest and promise of the women's movement opens up a new horizon for human development which touches the horizon of transcendence."[25] This horizon brings the movement into the range of religious studies and poses an important challenge for the future study of religion. As we begin to recover the voice of women in the religious life of humankind, we can move towards a richer apprehension of the spiritual life of humankind.

Raimundo Panikkar and the Cross-Cultural Study of Religion

Finally I want to mention, again all too briefly, the important work of Raimundo Panikkar. He was born in Spain of a Spanish mother and Indian father, educated both in the West and the East, and has divided his teaching between universities in the East and West. Retired from teaching at the University of California at Santa Barbara, he always spent a part of each year in India, often at Benares Hindu University. He is also a Catholic priest deeply committed to the Christian faith yet equally at home within the Vedic spiritually of the Hindu. Thus Panikkar transcends, as do all those I have discussed, the presumed dichotomy between the scholar and believer that was so pronounced in the modern study of religion. And, again like the others, there is a deep and abiding cross cultural, even cross religious, experience built into his life. Thus for Panikkar, the study of religion involves the experience, in the words of the Notre Dame theologian John Dunne, of "crossing over" into the spirituality of other traditions.

In his work *Intra-Religious Dialogue*, Panikkar charts some of the dynamics inherent in the process of coming to understand another tradition.[26] Here the task is not to explain—which has far too often been a process of "explaining away" by interpreting the religious practice or belief in terms alien to the tradition itself—but, as Heidegger said, to understand by standing under, by allowing the religious tradition to unfold in our consciousness in its own terms. Panikkar argues that in this process we find ourselves involved not in an inter-religious encounter, but in a dialogue within the religious heritage of humankind as such. This creative encounter Panikkar calls a "dialogic dialogue" wherein we, first, meet one another in an atmosphere of mutual openness, ready to alter misperceptions about the other and eager to appreciate the values of the other. Out of this first stage can arise a second stage in which we can be mutually enriched by passing over into the consciousness of the other so that each can experience to some degree the other's religiousness from within the other's perspective. Panikkar acknowledges that achieving this second stage, though possible, is very difficult. We then return to our own tradition renewed and made more aware of its own riches, but transformed by having shared the life of another.

Panikkar is intensely aware of the difficulties of articulating the meaning of the manifold spiritual paths to being religious because of the differing cultural contexts and patterns of meaning in each of the traditions. His warning needs to be heeded in the study of religion lest we draw conclusions that are too facile or superficial, or worse, add to the already vast amount of misunderstanding that exists between traditions. Thus a major virtue that the scholar of religion must cultivate is the capacity to listen, long and deeply, to the other. The scholar must return time and again to the text, the practice, the persons, the communities, always aware that we may grasp only in part, that there is always something more or deeper to be heard. Without this dialectical interior dialogue, as Panikkar calls it, our scholarship remains, at best, superficial—another item on the resume but not a contribution to religious understanding.

We in the West especially need to hear this criticism and to reformulate our approach to the study of religion to free it from the reductionism and ideological constraints that have been the dark side of our Enlightenment heritage. The figures I have discussed here can help us in that direction.

Let me conclude on another note. We live, as I said at the outset, in a time of growing planetary consciousness, but also in a time of recognition of the plurality of religious paths to be found in the human family. Both of these perceptions must be held together and brought more forcibly into our post-modern study of religion. What is also needed is a plurality of methods in the study of religion reflecting the diversity of the great traditions of scholarship that have been part of the non-Western cultures and traditions. Despite the growing numbers of peoples from outside the North Atlantic basin to be found in the West, we in the West still remain woefully ignorant of the great contributions of the civilizations and traditions of the East: the Middle East, India, Southeast Asia, China and Japan. And this ignorance is evident even in disciplines like Comparative Religion and Religious Studies. Moreover, we need to understand these traditions and civilizations in their own terms, terms that resonate deeply in the hearts and minds of the people from whom they emerged. My hope is that in the coming decades we will see work emerging from different parts of the world that moves beyond the limitations of the methods developed in the West, that drinks deeply at the life-giving sources of other traditions and cultures. Let me mention just two pioneers in such work. Dr. Krishna Sivaraman has provided us with an exemplary study of Saivism that leads us beyond the limits of Western scholarship on Eastern traditions. And Syyed Hossein Nasr's magnificent *Knowledge & the Sacred* deserves to be read by every scholar of religion. In addition to its intrinsic value, Nasr also articulates a critique of modern Western culture that very much needs to be heard in the West. It is a critique that is only possible from those who have followed another way, heard another voice, been nurtured by another cradle. May more scholarship like this be done in the future.

Endnotes

[1] S. Radhakrishnan, *Religion and Culture* (Delhi: Orient Paperbacks, 1968), 51.

[2] See Harold Remus et al., "Religious as an Academic Discipline," in *Encyclopedia of the American Religious Experience,* ed. C. H. Lippy and P. W. Williams (New York: Scribner's, 1988), 3:1653ff, for a standard account of the present state of Religious Studies in North America.

[3] Ninian Smart, *Beyond Ideology* (New York: Harper & Row, 1981), 47. Here I employ a three-fold distinction between traditional, modern, and post-modern study of religion.

[4] See also Stephen Crites lecture to the Society for Values in Higher Education entitled, "The Modernist Myth Exposed," which makes a similar point about the "modernist myth." The essay is available through *Soundings,* (Knoxville, TN: The University of Tennessee, 1990).

[5] Syed H. Nasr, *Sufi Essays* (London: G. Allen & Unwin, 1972), 128

[6] *Ibid.,* 127.

[7] See G. van der Leeuw, *Religion in Essence and Manifestation,* 2 vols. (New York: Harper and Row, 1963).

[8] See Walter Lippmann, *A Preface to Morals* (Boston: Beacon Press, 1929), 51ff.

[9] Nasr, *Sufi Essays,* 127.

[10] Mircea Eliade, *The Sacred and the Profane* (New York: Harper and Row, 1961).

[11] Mircea Eliade, *A History of Religious Ideas* (London: Collins, 1979), 1:xiii.

[12] Mircea Eliade, "Methodological Remarks on the Study of Religious Symbolism," in *The History of Religions: Essays in Methodology,* ed. M. Eliade and J. Kitagawa (Chicago: University of Chicago Press, 1959), 97.

[13] *Ibid.,* 97-98.

[14] *Ibid.,* 98.

[15] See the "Preface" in Huston Smith, *Forgotten Truth: The Primordial Tradition* (New York: Harper & Row, 1976), ixff. I have edited a collection of Smith's writings entitled *Huston Smith: Essays on World Religions* (St. Paul: Paragon, 1993).

[16] Ibid., 3.

[17] *Ibid.*, 34ff.

[18] *Ibid.*, 60.

[19] *Ibid.*, ix.

[20] See Wilfred Cantwell Smith, *The Meaning and End of Religion* (New York: New American Library, 1964).

[21] Wilfred Cantwell Smith, *The Faith of Other Men* (New York: New American Library, 1963), 17.

[22] Wilfred Cantwell Smith, *Towards a World Theology* (Philadelphia: Westminster Press, 1981), 3.

[23] *Ibid.*, 5-6.

[24] Ursula King, *Women and Spirituality, Voices of Protest and Promise* (London: Macmillian, 1989), 11. See also Ursula King, ed., *Women in the World's Religions, Past and Present* (New York: Paragon House, 1987).

[25] King, *Women and Spirituality*, 227.

[26] Raimundo Panikkar, *Intra-Religious Dialogue* (New York: Crossroads, 1978). See also my "Meeting at Snowmass: Some Dynamics of Interfaith Encounter," in *Interfaith Dialogue: Four Approaches*, ed. John Miller (Waterloo: University of Waterloo Press, 1986), 1-20.

[27] See Krishna Sivaraman, *Saivism in Philosophical Perspective* (Delhi: Motilal Banarsidas, 1973) and S. H. Nasr, *Knowledge and the Sacred* (Edinburgh: Edinburgh University Press, 1981).

II
Dynamics of Interfaith Encounter
and Dialogue

In the first essay I was concerned with clearing some ground for what I consider a new point of departure for the study of religion in our time: the living encounter between persons of differing faiths. This focus for the study of religion will, I believe, lead us beyond the limitations of what I called the "modern study of religion," that is, the approach to the study of religion that sought to understand religion in terms that were alien to religious consciousness itself. For if our point of departure is the living encounter between men and women of faith, then we will be spared the tendency to excessive abstraction, to easy generalization, to fitting the religious experience and beliefs of others into alien contests.

While one may believe that "Muslims are . . ." or that "Buddhists are . . .", it is intellectually dishonest to maintain such beliefs in the light of one's actual encounter with living members of a tradition other than one's own. Here in the encounter with men and women of other faiths, one is rather called upon to listen deeply in order to understand that complex experience, history, and tradition that makes the other what he or she is as well as that Beyond which founds their faith. Thus in this second essay I want to try to outline some of the presuppositions of the growing encounter and dialogue between persons of different faiths and the implications that arise from this encounter and dialogue for the study of religion in a new key.

The Priority of Event Over Reflection

Let me begin by attempting to describe, not as a neutral observer but as one involved and deeply affected, two events of meeting that have been part of my recent experience. I do this, first, in order to make clear my own conviction that the event of meeting, encounter, and dialogue must take precedence, for the student of religion, over the discussion of presuppositions for the interfaith encounter. The event has priority over considerations that emerge from academic study concerning what this event of meeting should or should not be, what issues should or should not be discussed. Such talk is whistling in the dark, a reversal of the proper order between religious life and its study. That study must be grounded in what is actually happening in the event of meeting itself. And second, the presuppositions of encounter and dialogue are those that are implicit within the event of meeting itself. It is thus in reflection upon the event of meeting that we discover, or can discover, what was presupposed and implicit in the meeting itself.

I have emphasized this point in order to underscore the fact that it is the event of meeting itself that is the new (not, of course, absolutely new but relatively in regard to its pervasiveness) factor in the religious situation of our time. This is the novel development in the history of religions that it is, in part, the task of the scholar of religion to explore and understand. It is the absence of meeting or the atmosphere of hostility when that encounter occurs that has been the major characteristic of the longer history of religion. But enough, let me turn to the events themselves.

As many of you are aware, it was my privilege in the 1980s and 1990s to have been involved in the organizing of a series of interreligious events. Especially important has been the series of conferences known as "God: The Contemporary Discussion."[1] In these meetings, we brought together scholars and believers from different traditions to contribute their

Bahubali, Jain Saint at Sravanabelagola,
Karnataka, South India

reflections on many different themes. In those conferences we have explored together such varied themes as "Spiritual Discipline & Ultimate Reality," "Naming God," "Women's Experience of the Divine," and "God, Nothing and the Ultimate."[2] The purpose of these meetings is not to come to definitive conclusions on these questions—an aim that is not only impossible but probably undesirable as well. Rather, our purpose was initiate a conversation within the planetary religious community concerning the Divine Mystery within which human life unfolds. While such meetings make the participants deeply aware of the differing patterns of understanding that Mystery found among the religious traditions of humankind, they also lead to a deepening desire to understand one another and what has been given to them in their respective traditions. In these meetings, which have now involved several hundreds of men and women, we were exploring the deepest grounds, the Ultimate Ground, of both our unity and difference, our difference and unity.

For several years, I was part of an interreligious Planning Committee that planned a series of meetings known as the Assembly of the World's Religions.[3] The first of these Assemblies was held in 1985 in McAfee, New Jersey, involving over 600 official participants and another few hundred spouses, children, staff, and visitors. This meeting sought to bring together a cross-section of persons from the different religious communities. Thus we had religious leaders as well as scholars, lay members, artists, men and women, young and old. Here the emphasis fell on interreligious sharing of one's spiritual journey as well as on reflection on one or another of the Assembly's twelve themes. Here we prayed and meditated together in addition to sharing ideas. Here we attempted in our small groups to become little outposts of caring and sharing in a world too much torn by conflict and mutual disregard. Here we gathered a token group of the world religious family: Muslims, Hindus, Taoists, Christians, Buddhists, Jews, Zoroastrians, Sikhs, Confucianists, Shintoists, African traditional religionists, and those who travel spiritual paths outside the named traditions. Over seven remarkable days, we prayed and played together in a virtual celebration of mutuality and difference that very much surprised us all— organizers as well as participants. Here, I believe, most of us recognized a spirit of unity that we could perhaps not adequately articulate, but that we could sense and out of which we could live. There followed further Assemblies of the World's Religions in 1990 in San Francisco and 1992 in Seoul, Korea. Similar was the 1993 Parliament of the World's Religions commemorating the 1893 Parliament in Chicago at the World's

Fair, an event that for the first time brought Eastern religions to the attention of many in the West.

I have described, albeit briefly and sketchily, these two events in my recent history and experience because they lie at the heart of my reflection on the presuppositions and implications of the living encounter between men and women of different faiths in our time. It is from these experiences of men and women from the different traditions meeting to pray together, to share their religious pilgrimages, to discuss and debate religious ideas and concepts, to explore together uncharted dimensions of the spirit, and to discover those common things shared across tradition as well as those distinctive things that give each tradition its special character and vocation that I have come to believe what I now believe about meeting, about dialogue from heart to heart. Thus what I want to do is to unpack some of the implicit assumptions resident in these events themselves and identify what seem to me to be the implications of such events for interreligious dialogue and study. This essay has something of the character of a voyage of discovery since I am sharing with you what I have learned.

Discovery One: Not Only Necessary But Desirable

We can approach the interreligious encounter in a number of ways. Many have spoken of this encounter as a necessity arising from the character of our participation in an emerging, to use Marshall McLuhan's phrase, "global village" or, in Ninian Smart's phrase, "global city."[4] This argument from necessity has much to commend it. As our planet grows smaller due to modern means of communication and travel, it is increasingly imperative that we understand one another if we are to live together in relative peace and harmony. And it is especially imperative that we understand the different cultures and religious traditions that have nurtured us from birth. But the argument from necessity is not sufficient in itself. It must be merged with its inner side, namely, the conviction that coming to know our planetary neighbours is not only necessary but desirable. The outer necessity needs to be linked to the heart's longing so that we can see, as well, how desirable it is for us to know the depths of the other. The encounter with one another is not only a necessity imposed from without, but an opportunity given us from within. Over the past several years, this truth has gradually dawned on me as I have been enriched and enlarged by meeting men and women from around the world who live out patterns of the religious life and experience of the Beyond that are not my own. This leads me to my second discovery.

Discovery Two: Not Only Tolerance But Appreciation

From the experience of meeting men and women from other traditions, one is led beyond tolerance to appreciation. It is, I believe, important to understand that out of genuine meeting grows something more than a reluctant tolerance of persons of other faiths, a grudging concession to the fact that others have not yet embraced our way. While tolerance is certainly a social good, it is only an intermediate stage on the road of genuine interreligious dialogue. In the encounter with men and women of different faiths, we are led, as have been the sages and wise ones of earlier ages, to a real appreciation of the gifts of other traditions. Every person will have different tales to tell at this point. In my experience, I think especially of my encounters with Tibetan Buddhists whose good humour and mental equanimity arise, I am persuaded, from their disciplines of meditation. Thus I find myself not only tolerating them, but actively appreciating them as having a real gift to share with the human family. Or I think of my encounters with Muslims who have urged me to "submit to Allah" and others who have given me a glimpse of the Sufi way. From each, something has been learned: from one, I have glimpsed an admirable depth of conviction, from the other, a glimpse of the mystic way that moves from the heart to embrace one gently. Thus I have found that one can move gradually from a recognition of the religiously plural situation of the human family to an active appreciation of the faith of others.

Discovery Three: Not Only Understanding But Transformation

In the living encounter of men and women of different faiths, one is not only led to deepen one's understanding of the other—a process that extends over time and is never finished—but one is truly transformed. We are transformed in a number of different ways and at different levels. At perhaps the most superficial but nevertheless important level, we are led to abandon our misconceptions of one another. We are led to overcome stereotypes and easy generalizations. People who have encountered others of different faiths abandon monolithic modes of speech that begin, "Hindus are ..." or "Jews are ..." or "Christians are ...". They appreciate more nuanced ways of speaking of others. We discover that just as we are aware of the range and variety of human sensibilities—and that people are at different stages in their own personal pilgrimages—to be found within our own community of faith, a similar range is to be found in other communities as well. When, for example, we Christians encounter the subtilities and depths of Vedanta, or the depth of bhakti to be found in a devotee of Krishna, it is impossible to retain the belief that all Hindus are mere "idol worshippers," as many Christians long believed. And as our understanding of the other grows and deepens, we are inwardly transformed as well. It is, of course, often difficult to trace the transformation in oneself. It is often recognized only with the passage of time or by one's friends, family and associates.

This transformation has led the critics of interreligious encounter to warn that such meeting will lead to a diminishment of faith, a loss of conviction, and a tendency to relativize all faiths. It would be as pointless to deny that in some cases this does happen as to pretend that the encounter

43

is not risky. It is risky, but equally risky for all who are truly involved. But the risk inherent in the encounter can lead in another direction as well: to a deepening and broadening of faith, to growth rather than disintegration. From my own experience I am persuaded that the negative prospects are greatly exaggerated, that they represent more an unfaced fear than a real danger. More common is the experience of an internal dialectic of transformation as one comes to understand his or her own faith anew in the context of the living faith of others. Although some have found in the "plurality of religious forms . . . an argument against the validity of all religions," I find myself in agreement with Professor S. H. Nasr that "the most powerful defence for religion . . . is precisely the universality of religion."[5] In the living encounter, this later response is more common: out of the encounter with the living faith of others, one is encouraged to deepen one's own faith. This is often another transforming consequence of meeting men and women of other faiths.

Discovery Four: Not Empty But Open

When asked about the presuppositions of interreligious dialogue, I have always replied that, in my experience, there is only one prerequisite for dialogue: openness to the other. But this does not mean that we come empty to the interreligious encounter. We rather come as men and women formed by different traditions and different patterns of religious life. Even when our religious practice may be very cursory, we continually discover that we carry with us at least the cultural forms that have emerged from the religious traditions that formed our cultures. Paul Tillich reminded us that "culture is the form of religion, religion is the substance of culture." This dialectical interplay between religion and culture is something we need to grasp more fully, and it is readily apparent in the interreligious encounter. On the personal level, we need not, nor is it possible, to come to the encounter empty handed. Rather, we come as members of religious traditions, as men and women of faith, though to varying degrees. We come bearing the accumulated burdens and virtues of our traditions of faith, of learning, of culture, of ritual, and of personal experience. And these carry with them, let me emphasize, burdens and limitations as well as gifts. Most of us, for example, carry the suspicion—I know this was true for myself—that those in other traditions are not as blessed, favoured, or enlightened as those in our tradition. And it may turn out to be an accurate suspicion in certain respects. But more often, it is a spiritual obstacle to be overcome if one is truly to be open to the other.

Thus while I believe that the single thing required for interreligious dialogue is openness to the other, I am convinced that this is truly one of the most difficult spiritual states to achieve. As I have said, this state must grow not out of our internal emptiness, but out of the depth of out rootedness in particular traditions, ways of practice, and habits of prayer and meditation. It is from these depths that one can come to be in relation to the Divine Ground of things given in one's tradition and thus truly be open to the other. Rootedness in a given tradition is not, in my experience, an obstacle to openness to the other, but the spiritual presupposition of openness. For from such rootedness one can relate to the other out of serenity rather than apprehension, out of inward rest rather than desperate longing. As a Christian, for example, I must come to see the other with love; as a Buddhist, with compassion; as a Hindu, with identity. In this spiritual condition, one's faith is not external, nor is one's religion. Rather, they have become our way to life as well as our way of life. Here one can see the other not as a threat but as a fellow pilgrim.

At the moral level, openness to the other is manifest as a willingness to be corrected and instructed by the other. For here we have passed from morality as outward rules to the moral life as the pathway to goodness. On the intellectual level, openness to the other is manifest as a love of the truth, however it comes to us. Here, we intellectuals and scholars often have a great deal of difficulty! We often believe ourselves to have the truth, and thus there is no need for us to listen, only for the other to listen to us. Or we are often so wedded to our own conceptualizations that we are reluctant to truly hear others and to enter into their mental landscape. Thus it is imperative that intellectual openness be achieved in the process of dialogue itself. And again, I do not mean emptiness, but a willingness to see our own views as perhaps a little less than the truth itself, as an attempt to articulate a mystery that always remains, in part, beyond our schemes and thinking. At the same time, it is crucial that we offer one another our best and deepest thinking and insight, that we share what we believe has been given to us in the intellectual traditions of our community. Only in this way can we move ahead, or rework or revise our traditions if necessary. (For example, many of us who have been burdened by an excessive rationalism or an arid intellectualism need to be reminded, as is so clear in the great Hindu traditions, of the links between self-realization and thought, between spiritual practice and thinking).

Hence while we do not come empty to the encounter of men and women of different faiths, we must learn to cultivate a multidimensional openness to the other, for it is only from such openness that monologues can be transformed into genuine dialogue.

Discovery Five: Not Multiple Monologues But Genuine Dialogue

Too often, the encounter of men and women of different faiths is what might be called "multiple monologues," persons speaking to themselves in sequential order or side by side. We are thus presented with "The Christian View" followed by "The Hindu View" followed by "The Muslim View," etc. In this situation, we have not really encountered one another, nor have we truly met or entered into genuine dialogue. As Srivatsa Goswami regularly reminds me: dialogue is dangerous. He is right. Because in genuine dialogue, where we are truly open to one another, we will be changed. What will change is both our perception of the other and our own religious self-understanding. While people come to the encounter of persons of living faiths with what has been given to them of the Divine in their respective traditions, they discover in dialogue that what has been given does not exhaust the fullness of Divine Life, that there is an inexhaustible More that we can be led into through the dialogue with persons of other traditions. It is extremely difficult to know precisely how to articulate this point, since I do not mean to suggest either (a) that any particular religious path is an inadequate way to the fullness of the Divine, nor (b) that we are led to a new syncretism. But I do want to say that no tradition exhausts the fullness of Divine Life.

This is of course an emergent insight that arises in dialogue itself as the very ground and presupposition of dialogue. What made the coming together, the genuine meeting itself, possible, now emerges as the ground of all subsequent meeting. Thus I prefer to say that in dialogue we rediscover ourselves as fellow pilgrims who have come from various places but who, in the process of meeting and sharing, recognize both similarities and differences in relation to a shared aspiration to live out of the multiform richness of divine life. In dialogue the Christian knows himself or herself anew in a fellowship of believers that not only includes other Christians, but other believers in other traditions as well. The Muslim remains a Muslim but wonders at the variety of Allah's presence in the lives of others. The Hindu remains a Hindu but delights in the manifold expressions of the One who is beyond all expressions. And yet each of us in our own way is moved to be Christian or Muslim or Buddhist or Hindu in ways that we were not before. And it is here that the transforming quality of genuine dialogue occurs. This transformation is what the American Christian Ruel Howe, in another context, called "the miracle of dialogue."[6]

Some prefer a name other than dialogue for the living encounter between persons of different faiths.[7] For example, Wilfrid Cantwell Smith speaks about the interreligious colloquy, and others speak of a "multilog" since more than two (dia-) are involved. But I prefer the term dialogue because it more adequately points to the central issue and dynamic: the encounter of a speaker and listener, a listener and a speaker, in the process of communing one with another in relation to a ground that precedes and sustains them. And it is in the miracle of communication becoming communion that we encounter the true heart of genuine dialogue, of genuine meeting. The whole person is affected: not only our understanding but our hearts as well, not only our minds but our spirits too. Thus we are led to discovery six.

Discovery Six: Not Only Change But Growth

If dialogue has something of the quality I have suggested above, then we discover that the encounter with the other is not merely an occasion for change but an opportunity for growth, a call to become more. In religious terms, the encounter leads to spiritual growth. As we encounter the richness of another tradition—its patterns of piety and thought, of ritual and life, of discipline and devotion—we are led more deeply into the resources of our own traditions and can see and appropriate them in a new light. Thus we not only change but we grow and become more. For one so deeply affected by the interreligious encounter, this transformation now seems obvious, but at the outset one might anticipate only loss and change. One might approach dialogue with misgiving. Let me report from inside the encounter that there are real possibilities for growth.

It is of course impossible to characterize that growth in any singular way except to say that it involves a greater appropriation of the universal elements of our particular traditions. Growth will be varied depending on where one is on the spiritual journey when one comes into this living encounter. But that one will experience growth is, I am persuaded, a virtual corollary of genuine meeting.

Discovery Seven: Not a New Syncretism But a Revitalized Family of Religious Pathways

Some have feared that out of the living encounter of persons of different faiths will arise a new syncretism that will blur the distinctions between the different religious traditions. But this fear leads us back to the very fundamental issue of the nature of religion itself. What is the end or goal of religious life? While this is a hotly debated issue in the study of religion, my own conviction is that religion is the quest to relate human to divine life. Thus religious life is a means towards the fullness of our humanity. While religions differ in fundamental ways in their accounts of both the human and divine, they are all agreed that it is only in relation to a Beyond that transcends the mundane that we come into our fullness as human beings. For example, in some strands of Hinduism we are called to recognize the fundamental identity of "atman" with "brahman," in others we are called to a life of devotion or bhakti. In some Buddhist traditions, we are enjoined to practice a meditative middle way which will lead us beyond suffering to enlightenment. In some Christian traditions, we are urged to a life of the love of God and our neighbour as exemplified in Jesus Christ. In the Islamic traditions, we are called to submit to Allah as the source of our true freedom. And so on and so forth. What thus emerges in the religious life of humankind is a variety of divine/human types that each tradition, through its practice, beliefs, and life, nurtures. Religions, then, are nurseries for distinctive human types.

In this perspective, then, the end of the living encounter between persons of the different traditions is not a new syncretism. Rather, it is a synchronizing of the pathways of the different types in relation to their divine ground. From my own experience of interreligious dialogue, I am not persuaded either that "all religions are the same," or that "the

49

differences are merely superficial." At the same time, I am persuaded that we have much to share across tradition and, perhaps paradoxically, that we have more in common than we normally recognize. But the issue is where to locate those shared things, those things held in common. It is clear to me that they do not lie in the specifics of ritual, or belief, or practice, or prayer, or meditation, or scriptures, of any other of the specifics of a given tradition; they lie in the shared reality of believing, praying, meditating, reading scriptures, acting out rituals, and practicing the spiritual life and disciplines. These are common or shared dimensions of our varied pathways that lift human into divine life, of our being met by divine life in the midst of the human pilgrimage. This is a crucial point. While a Muslim prays to Allah, a Christian to the Triune God, a Hindu to Krishna or Ram, etc., they all have the common experience of prayer. And while one may believe in her Guru, another in her Dharma and yet another in the Tao, they all have the shared experience of believing. And it is precisely here that we find the grounds to recognize one another as fellow pilgrims, though on different pathways, perhaps to different specific ends, and surely with different maps of the Beyond (if not different Beyonds). But it is in our shared experience of believing, praying, meditating, and doing that we can as religious pilgrims meet one another; it is here that we discover our human unity as pilgrims.

Over these past few years I have walked with pilgrims in Vrindaban and Varanasi, I have prayed with Muslims in mosques in Delhi, and I have meditated with Buddhists in Dharamsala. It would be not only presumptuous but wrong to say either that I understand them in the way they understand themselves, or that we are all engaged in precisely the same thing in those shared moments. And yet I believe that it is precisely because I am attempting to walk in the Christian way that I can share, in part, their experience, understand, in part, what they are doing, be present, in part, to their world. And vice versa. Nor do I believe it would be a

Golden Temple, Sikh Holy Place, Amritsar, Punjab, India

gain if I were to become a Hindu or a Muslim, or if they were to become Christians. Rather, I am persuaded that we all gain to the extent that we share across traditions how we are becoming human/divine in the religious pathways that we each walk. And we gain by learning how to make those gifts more present to the world in the service of a broken human family. Thus the end of the interreligious encounter is a revitalized family of religious pathways, each nourished by what has been given to it, willing to be nurtured in the distinctive type each is, and yet open to sharing across traditions those common religious experiences and gestures of prayer, meditation, discipline, ritual, reflection, and service. Much more important than syncretism is the need to encourage the universal dimensions of each tradition that they might come to cooperate with one another in service to humanity. And for that service we need a symphony of types, human types nurtured by the respective genius of each

51

tradition, yet willing to share their virtues and gifts with others. Thus the human as well as the theological dimensions must be—and are being—fruitfully sychronized with one another.

There are, to be sure, few to whom one can point as examples of the type that might emerge from the interreligious encounter. But I think here of great souls like Gandhiji, so fully Hindu yet so open to other traditions, so fully himself yet so transparent to a Beyond that sustained him. Or of Mother Theresa, so fully Christian yet so fully radiant that we can all recognize our deepest aspirations in her. Or of the Dali Lama, so fully Buddhist yet with a warmth and compassion that is so truly human. And on a less dramatic scale, there are those men and women who are finding in the living encounter with men and women of different faiths the crucible for their own movement into the depths of own their tradition as the way into the universal human family, a revitalized family of religious pathways to the Beyond.

Discovery Eight: Not Uniformity But Mutuality

Thus what emerges in the living encounter is not uniformity, nor a levelling to a lowest common denominator. Rather, we are led into new and unanticipated forms of mutuality and cooperation. Too often our religious nurseries have been places to hide to avoid coming to grips with the real problems that everywhere face our world. But the interreligious encounter and dialogue leads, it seems to me, in another direction: it leads towards the renewal of religious life and a more fruitful encounter with the world. I think here of the World Conference for Religion and Peace, to mention but one example. Here persons from many traditions are attempting to find forms of mutuality and cooperation that encourage not only interreligious understanding but worldly action as well. Thus, finally, we come to discovery nine.

Discovery Nine: We Are Sustained in Interreligious Dialogue by a Beyond that is Beyond all Our reckoning

Let me mention finally the most difficult point to articulate, but the most important point to make—namely, that in the living encounter of men and women of different faiths, we are sustained by a Beyond beyond all our reckoning. When the miracle of dialogue occurs—and those moments cannot be pre-programmed or pre-packaged—we gain a glimpse of that Beyond that exceeds all our conceptions and prejudgments, all our carefully crafted rituals and theologies, all the differences that unite us. That Beyond I call Love, but others would name it in other ways. It matters not. What matters is that we acknowledge it, that we say yes when it comes, for here we are touched by *grace*, here we have glimpsed the *mystery* in which it all unfolds, here, in the language of my tradition, *"We have seen through a glass darkly."*

Thus at the end of this voyage of discovery we are led back to the beginning: the presupposition of the interreligious encounter and dialogue is that we find ourselves in the midst of a transcendent mystery that continually exceeds us yet makes itself known in ways that can heal and transform the human family. This is the ground that was lurking there at the beginning of the voyage, but we could not yet see it because we had not left the shore. But once we go, then we can see what has been present all along, waiting to make itself manifest to the voyagers. Just as our planet has always been a blue orb spinning through the endless mystery, so it took the voyage to the moon to allow us to see it. Yet we are still far from realizing all of what it means. So too the interreligious dialogue in our time is just beginning, and we are now beginning to get some reports of what lies ahead. Yet we are still a long way from knowing fully its meanings and implications.[8] Indeed, we need to be patient to allow the seeds that have been sown to take root and grow up into their proper forms. We must not attempt to force the fruit prematurely; it must be allowed to ripen into its own proper end.

Our way into this voyage is through the lifeboat of our own traditions since these are the living vehicles that have transported countless numbers before us from the shores of birth to the other shore of death. They thus merit our continued loyalty and devotion, not as ends in themselves, but because they lead us to ends beyond themselves. We can walk on these paths because they have been trodden before, and they are the best preparation for travelling on new terrain. In the interreligious dialogue of our time, some new paths are emerging, but they are just being pioneered. Fortunately, we are finding that there were wise mothers and fathers who have already gone ahead of us—and we can learn from them. And at the same time, we are discovering that the patterns of religious isolation that have been too much a part of the long history of religions are beginning to breakdown. And here lies the story that, in large part, it is the task and responsibility of the scholar of religion today to try to understand. That scholar will begin this task armed with the best historical, social scientific, psycho-spiritual, and religious methods available. She will have to do battle with the perverse secularism that has too much infected us precisely for the sake of the secular. There the scholar of religion will learn to do comparative religion in a new key. But the scales, tones, and ends of that new key will have to wait till my next essay.

Endnotes

[1] The interreligious meetings known as "God: The Contemporary Discussion" were initiated in 1981 through the New Ecumenical Research Association (New ERA), New York, New York, USA. There were eight meetings in this series. The final conference in this series was held in France in 1992, Dr. Francis D'Sa of Pune, India was the Chair.

[2] From these meetings twenty volumes appeared. The entire series, known as "God: The Contemporary Discussion," is

available from Paragon House, 2700 University Avenue West, St. Paul, Minnesota, USA 55114. Among the titles are James Duerlinger, ed., *Ultimate Reality and Spiritual Discipline* (1984); F. Ferre and R. Mataragnon, eds., *God and Global Justice* (1985); M. D. Bryant and R. Mataragnon, eds., *The Many Faces of Religion and Society* (1985); R. Scharlemann and Gilbert Ogutu, eds., *Naming God* (1986); Ursula King, ed., *Women in the World's Religions* (1987); and H. Ruf, *Religion, Ontotheology, and Deconstruction* (1989).

I was the Senior Consultant for New ERA and part of the Executive Committee for the Assemblies of the World's Religions. I was the series editor for the volumes coming from the "God Conferences." Thus, I have been intimately involved in the process of planning these conferences and the resultant publications.

[3] The first Assembly of the World's Religions (AWR) was held in 1985; the second occurred in August, 1990, in San Francisco, California, USA; the third in Seoul, Korea in 1992. For a fuller account of the first assembly, see M. D. Bryant, J. Maniatis, and T. Hendricks, eds., *Assembly of the World's Religions, 1985: Spiritual Unity and the Future of the Earth* (New York: International Religious Foundation, 1986), volumes from the subsquent assemblies are also available.

[4] See Ninian Smart, *Beyond Ideology* (New York: Harper & Row, 1981), 22.

[5] S. H. Nasr, *Sufi Essays* (London: G. Allen & Unwin, 1972), 126.

[6] Ruel L. Howe, *The Miracle of Dialogue* (New York: Seabury Press, 1963). I have now forgotten much of the content of his book, but the title stayed with me.

[7] For something of this discussion see, for example, Paul Knitter, *No Other Name? A Critical Survey of Christian Attitudes Towards the World Religions* (Maryknoll, NY: Orbis Books, 1985).

[8] There are many important volumes on this subject now available. One of the most important is Diana Eck, *Encountering God: From Bozeman to Benares* (Boston: Beacon Press, 1993). My own contribution to this literature is M. Darrol Bryant and Frank K. Finn, eds., *Interreligious Dialogue: Voices From a New Frontier* (New York: Paragon House, 1989); Darrol Bryant and S. A. Ali, *Muslim Christian Dialogue: Problems and Promise* (St. Paul: Paragon House, 1998) and M. Darrol Bryant, *Woven on the Loom of Time: Many Faiths and One Divine Purpose* (New Delhi: Suryodaya/Decent Books, 1999).

III
Notes Towards the Symphony
of Living Faiths

In the first essay of this volume I sought to clear some ground for a new approach to the study of religion, one that would take as its point of departure the emerging dialogue in our own time between men and women of different faiths. I have urged this point of departure in order to underscore the priority of the lived experience of religious life over its study. Our study as scholars of religion must be subject to the actualities of lived experience within the religious traditions themselves rather than to methodological assumptions that are foreign to the phenomenon of religious life. In my second essay I shifted voice from that of a historian of religions to a more personal voice in offering an account of the dynamics of interfaith meeting and dialogue. In that essay my concern was to go beyond the external study of religion and move within the living encounter of men and women of different faiths in our own time. What emerges from that approach is an awareness of the (a) different religious pathways to be found among men and women of different faiths and, simultaneously, (b) an awareness of the cross-tradition mutuality that arises from the shared experience of believing, living, praying, acting, and practising what is given in one's tradition. In this third essay, I wish to turn to the implications of this living encounter of men and women of different faiths for the study of religion in general, to outline that study in a new key.

Religious Studies and Comparative Studies

As I observed in my first essay, the study of religion is a recent development in the intellectual history of humankind. Of course, this statement needs to be qualified in the sense that in the last century there emerged a "science of religion" that sought to be historical, descriptive, and analytic. This approach to the study of religion has led to a quantum jump in available information on the various religious traditions found in the human family. The gains are great. However, that study was also profoundly limited. The limitations arose, in large part, from a model of science that was inadequate to the religious phenomena themselves. In a word, the model obscured the role of the subject in the study of religion, the place of imaginative identification with the other as a prerequisite to understanding, and the ontological dimensions of religious experience that were in conflict with the scientism of the dominant method of study. This has led, at least in North America, to a continuing debate between those who champion an "objective science of religion" and those who see the study of religion as part of "humanistic studies." This is, I believe, a misplaced debate.

The study of religion is not a science in the sense of the natural sciences, but it is a science in the broader sense of "a disciplined way of proceeding" that has as its end the understanding of the variety of religious traditions as pathways of transcendence. Thus the study of religion is a discipline in its own right that is not reducible to history or sociology or psychology or even theology, as important as these disciplines are to the study of religion. What distinguishes the study of religion from the other disciplines is precisely its willingness to take seriously the religious dimensions of human life and experience and, most centrally, the dimension of living in relation to a Beyond that is itself beyond the methodological grasp of the discipline. At the same time, the study of religion is a humanistic enterprise precisely because it is the study of

57

human beings, men and women in communities and traditions of faith, as *homo religious*.

In this view, then, the study of religion is vast, encompassing the whole range of human experience of the Beyond as it is manifest in whole cultures and civilizations past and present, in communities and traditions of faith, in patterns of piety and practice, belief and gesture. The comparative study of religion is both an aspect of this larger study of religion and a particular area of study aimed at the comparison of traditions and of particular beliefs, practices, rituals, etc. across traditions. In recent decades, as many of you are aware, comparative study has come under considerable criticism. That criticism has been directed towards two tendencies. First, there is the tendency for comparative study to degenerate into apologetics by comparing the strength of one's own tradition with the weakness of another, or to caricature the other. This misuse of comparative religion is quickly dismissed by the community of scholars of religion, but much mischief can occur here. The second, more serious criticism, is against the superficiality of much comparative study. Here the tendency is to string together scattered texts from different sacred literatures or quotations from different religious writers in order to show a presumed agreement or disagreement between traditions. Again, this is a procedure unworthy of a scholar of religion. But beyond these criticisms there is a role for comparative study, a role that Professor Vahiddudin of the Indian Institute of Islamic Studies describes as creating an ethos and environment of understanding and respect for the meeting of persons of different traditions.[1] Taking this note as a point of departure, then, let me turn to some of the notes for the study of religion in a new key.

The Musical Metaphor: A Word of Explanation

I call this series of essays "Religion in a New Key." My emphasis does not fall on the "key" that unlocks doors, though I do hope that what I say will open some vistas on the study

Dancing figures from the Halebid Temple, Karnataka, South India

of religion. Rather, my emphasis falls on the musical metaphor of "key" as a tone that will permeate the study of religion. And that key involves, in discursive terms, a constellation of notes that add up to a new sensitivity to the variety of ways that the religious life has been lived, a willingness to hear anew the many songs that have been played in the cosmic dance. Such a metaphor has, of course, its limitations, but it also has its multivalent suggestiveness. Part of its suggestiveness may lie in the importance I give in the study of religion to the imagination, to intuition, to playful identification with the other, to a willingness to learn to sing the other's song. The study of religion is not only, or even primarily, an exercise of technical reason, but it is, in the first instance, the exercise of disciplined imagination. Religious life as a lived response to the Ultimate has more in common with music than with discursive or technical reason that seeks to master what is. And thus the student of religion must cultivate the sensitivities of a singer and dancer, as much if not more than those of an analyst and philosopher, if she is rightly to appropriate her subject. Let me try to indicate some of those

Halebid Temple, Karnataka, South India

notes for the study of religion in a new key in the hope that harmony rather than dissonance results.

Note Number One: The Transcendent Ground Tone

Fundamental to the study of religion is the encounter with the conviction, variously conceptualized and articulated but universally present, that we live in relation to a Beyond that exceeds the mundane world. This conviction has been problematic to the modern study of religion, leading many to believe that this central element of religious life must be "bracketed" in the study of religion. Ninian Smart, one of the most outstanding students of religion today, has written concerning the transcendent that

> . . . this does not mean that we have to believe in the transcendent in order to conduct the history of religions, or in order to construct a theory of the way religion works.[2]

While this is certainly a complex issue, it seems to me that such a position is methodologically untenable for the study of religion. Smart himself acknowledges how central the transcendent is to the history of human religiousness. And he is surely right in noting that there is no particular belief in the transcendent that is a requirement for the study of religion and that historical and sociological studies of religion can leave this question aside. But I find it difficult to understand how we in the study of religion can so easily dismiss this matter. While we do not have to decide if this or that belief about the Transcendent is true, it seems to me indispensable for the study of religion that we proceed, at least, as if the Transcendent, however understood in the different traditions, is. Moreover, it seems to me that a further conviction concerning a transcendent Beyond is not an impediment but an aid in the study of religion because it provides a point of entry into the living experiences of the other. The study of religion involves, in large measure, as Smart himself acknowledges, a disciplined empathy, a capacity, in the words of the first Nations of North America, to "walk in another's moccasins." And if the moccasins we are asked to walk in include a belief in a Beyond, then our "bracketing" of that dimension will make it virtually impossible to truly enter into the pattern of religiousness that we find in the other. Thus it seems to me imperative that we distinguish attempting to "prove" the truth or falsity of a particular belief in the Beyond from the methodological requirement in the study of religion to proceed on the assumption that the believer's experience of what is, including the Beyond, is true. Thus I would argue that we need to reverse the "bracketing process" and see that in the study of religion, we can only proceed on the methodological principle of acknowledging the transcendent as central to the human believers it is our task to understand.

When our point of departure is the living encounter of men and women of different faiths, this issue becomes even more acute. In the presence of believers, the student of religion will be challenged to explore his or her own faith or lack thereof. Faithfulness to the subject will require the student to acknowledge such faith as part of the lives he or she is trying to understand. But it may well lead one into what we might call the study of "comparative Beyonds," the ways in which believers or pilgrims on different religious paths map the Beyond they recognize as the true source of their life. Such an enterprise is exceedingly complex and difficult because the religious life comes as a whole life, and thus to abstract those comparative maps of the beyond may lead to distortion. Yet in the hands of the true artist in the study of religion, such a task is possible as can be seen in the masterworks of the great practitioners of the discipline.[3] Moreover, the student of religion is led to see something of the Transcendent Mystery that comes to view in the living encounter of men and women of different faiths. Taking this living dialogue as the point of departure, he or she is placed in the heart of this Transcendent mystery which is the ground tone for the study in a new key. It is, finally, sensitivity to the manifold songs played by the Transcendent in the lives of human beings that is the mark of the scholar of religion. This observation immediately opens up the second note of the new key for comparative religion.

Note Number Two: The Manifold Melodies, or the Variety of Pathways and Their Multiformity

If one turns to the study of religion from the context of the living encounter of men and women of different faiths, one is immediately aware of the manifold melodies that have come to expression in the history of religions/religion. At first blush, the manifold number is overwhelming. It includes not only all the great traditions such as Hinduism, Taoism, Buddhism, etc.,—but all the multiform traditions within the great traditions as well as the smaller traditions. No single mind can comprehend this variety in all its detail, or even in its sheer number. Instead, we must recognize the need to create a community of scholarship, a community of men and women devoted to the attempt to understand the manifold melodies of the religious life. Most often, we begin our studies by attempting to understand the tradition out of which we came, but some are also attracted to the study of traditions that are not their own. What moves us in one or another direction is often difficult to know, but at bottom there must be some passion to understand the dynamics present in a given tradition. Otherwise, the vocation to scholarship becomes a mere job, a love of the truth sold for a handful of pottage. But if our scholarship remains rooted in the love of our subject, then we will be at great pains to present its contour and shape with loving care, to disclose its inward melody with great precision and fidelity, to be faithful to the text or tradition or person or movement or ritual that we are seeking to understand.

The student of comparative religion thus undertakes his or her work against the backdrop of the manifold melodies of religious life—and within the context of a community of scholarship. Yet any single scholar will probably be able to truly master only one major or minor key in that larger symphony of religious pathways. Here lies the change that has taken place in recent decades in the study of religion, namely, that one's work will be read by other scholars and by living members of that particular tradition on which one works. This new audience has led a scholar like Wilfrid Cantwell Smith to remind us that "it is the business of comparative religion to construct statements about religion that are intelligible within at least two traditions simultaneously."[4] For example, our work must be such that a Muslim is able to acknowledge what a Christian writes about Islam, or a Buddhist what a Hindu writes about Buddhism. We are all being drawn into a planetary conversation that has considerable significance for comparative studies. Because if we in the study of religion can find ways to communicate one with another across the differences of tradition, language, culture, and especially ultimate commitments, then we might hope that such communication can take place in other spheres of life as well.

Equally important, contributors to the study of religion who come from outside the so-called "Western" world will do much to overcome the secular rationalism that has been the secret religion of so much religious study in the last hundred years. For as Buddhists write on Christian traditions, Hindus on Jewish traditions, and Muslims on Taoist traditions, we will begin to overcome the limitations of the Western secular rationalist bias in the study of religion.

At the same time, we must be aware of the limitations of comparative study: while we can establish commonalities across traditions, we must beware of too easily seeing identities. Each tradition is a complete and distinct melody of its own, with each note gaining its particular resonance and distinctiveness in relation to that whole melody. Thus to compare traditions as if the presence of the same or similar notes in each is equivalent to establishing the identity of the two traditions is not only bad musicology but it is bad comparative religion. In other words, the question of the one and the many, or of unity and difference, must be approached with great caution and only out of a deep awareness and appreciation of the distinctive melody or melodies present in a given tradition. To observe, for example, that there are certain similarities, or at least comparative possibilities, between Luther's doctrine of "faith alone" and the emphasis on "faith alone" found in certain forms of Pure Land Buddhism, especially Nichiren, is both suggestive and misleading. Each doctrine understood in the fullness of the respective traditions in which it stands, means quite different things. And yet to note such parallels can be illuminating. Thus there is the constant danger of superficial comparisons suggested by analogies of language or terminology, rather than of substance. Thus we should be at great pains to acknowledge the differences in the very process of comparing, for example, "faith" in the different traditions. Without the dialectic of similarity and difference as a constitutive part of religious studies we fall either into a simplistic identification or into sheer multiplicity. Thus I prefer the term "the multiform traditions" as a way of suggesting the essential point: religiousness comes in multiple forms, but they are still forms of religiousness. We can respect the manifold melodies while still recognizing their kindred character as expressions of the Transcendent Musician.

Indeed, a major task of the comparative study of religion is to disclose the different ways in which the same or similar terms are used, meant and understood in different traditions. For example, an examination of the term "prophet" as it appears and has come to be understood in Jewish, Christian, and Islamic traditions reveals more differences in meaning than similarities. And such an investigation might contribute considerably to understanding between these traditions. Thus comparative study often moves within the context or against the backdrop of identity and difference, attempting both to respect the integrity of the particular traditions and to show commonalities (if not identities) across traditions.

Note Number Three: The Human Notes of a Traditon's Melody

When asked about his religion, Gandhiji replied, "You must watch my life, how I live, eat, sleep, talk, behave in general. The sum total of all these in me is my religion."[5] It is important as students of religion to be reminded that religion is something lived, something manifest, in the deeply religious and culturally religious, in the whole range of a human beings being and doing. We must remember that religion comes embodied in the lives of human beings who are, finally, the human focus of our study. Religion, as Wilfrid Cantwell Smith has observed, is more concerned with the study of persons than "its," abstractions that we label Hinduism, Buddhism, etc. This is a crucial point for the student of religion to recall, and it is never far from consciousness if we make the living encounter of persons of different faiths the point of departure for comparative study. Here we are immediately confronted by the human notes of the tradition one wants to understand. It is not Hinduism as such—a notion that every Hindu I have ever met rejects—but Shrivatsa, and Dr. Balasubramaniam, and those pilgrims going from temple to temple in Vrindaban, or bathing in the Ganges at Benares, that we seek to understand. It is the Muslims we met on the street as well as in the Mosque, at learned conferences or on pilgrimage to Mecca that are the human notes and faces of the tradition. Every tradition has a more popular as well as a more learned face, a more textual as well as a more behavioural side, inward dynamics as well as outward institutions. And all of these have to be expressed in the process of understanding one another. All of these have contributed to the formation of the persons who call themselves Muslims or Hindus or Christians or Jews or Buddhists, but even all taken together they do not make the mystery of another person's lived religiousness any less profound.

Thus though we in the profession of the study of religion can be pleased with the information on the religious life that we have gathered, even with some of the theories we have constructed, we must even be more conscious of how little we understand the complexities of the human religious psyche, or institutions, or the dynamics of piety, or the subtleties of texts. We can not now, nor will we ever be able to say that we have explained religion, we can only make some limited progress in understanding what comes to expression in human beings as the traditions are lived from generation to generation. The reason for my sense of the limitations of our study is not just related to the limits of rational inquiry but also to the conviction that has grown in me through the study of religion that human life is only partially available to us, that human lives are rooted in a Beyond, an Ultimacy, that always exceeds the measure of our methods. And yet I would not underestimate the importance of our work, only note its limits.

The student of religion is not only concerned to understand the externals of religious life, its institutions, its postures of prayer and meditation, its texts and theologies, its actions and history, but how each of these interfaces with the within of the religious person, what we call the "life of faith." In understanding that great within we are again and again brought face to face with the mystery of the human person, especially of those persons who believe the within is linked to a Beyond. Let me turn again to the figure of Gandhi. In the recent film of Gandhi, so widely praised (and justifiably so), we encounter the political Gandhi, the leader of movements that led to the independence of India. But what was missing here, I felt, was a sense of the inward spiritual dynamic that funded and pervaded his acts. For that we must turn to an outstanding study like Margaret Chatterjee's *Gandhi's Religious Thought* [6] which brings us more in touch with that great within of this man's life, with what he called in his autobiography, *The Story of My Experiments with Truth*. [7] In this example we can perhaps see something of the multiformity of the religious person, that they come from somewhere (have a history), are formed by institutions and practices (have an outer front), have an interior life of prayer, meditation and inwardness (have an inner front), and a forward front of aspiration, hope and dreams. And as we approach the multiform human being we have to see how these dimensions of their life are rooted in a Beyond if we are to grasp them aright, or even in part. [8]

Thus the human notes of religious life gain their resonance and fullness by their rootedness in the Beyond as that is given to them in the twistings and turnings of their living experience. And this must always be remembered by the student of religion.

Note Number Four: Dissonance and Discord, Conflict between Religions

Throughout these essay I have emphasized the positive aspects of the living encounter between men and women of different faiths. But it must also be acknowledged that dissonance and discord are equally part of this living encounter. Beliefs and practices are perceived to conflict, antagonisms rooted in the long histories of conflict between traditions surface, mistrust continually manifests itself. Here again I believe that the scholar of religion has an important role to play in examining the roots and nature of this dissonance and discord, of helping persons and communities to sort out these conflicts in which the scholar himself (or herself) is often involved. The comparative study of religion can contribute to this process of mutual understanding by providing that forum for reasoned examination. In the West one thinks for example or especially of the long and bitter relations between the Jewish and Christian communities. What progress there has been overcoming some aspects of this long and bitter history has been made by those who have risked dialogue and by scholars in both traditions who have been willing to reexamine their own traditions on this point. From this process, many (but still too few) Christians have been led beyond the caricatures of Jews and theological prejudices that have too long been part of the Christian heritage.

One might hope for similar developments within India, and there have been some, — for example, the Indian Institute of Islamic Studies research on "Inter-religious Perceptions of Hindus and Muslims" in 1982, as well as Gandhi's own example—as the way to lessen, if not overcome, communal tensions.[9] Surely this is needed around the planet: in the Middle East, Ireland, Sri Lanka, South Africa and everywhere where religious differences are believed to be a source of dissonance rather than harmony. Here the scholar of religion who is also a believer in a particular religious community can make a significant contribution by being a person within that community who urges understanding rather than continued conflict, who can show that genuine differences can have creative rather than conflictual consequences.

Again the contributions of the scholar of religion to overcoming dissonance and discord will be modest. But at least she should attempt to bring the light of understanding to this area in the hope that greater degrees of understanding—without asserting anything about the ultimate compatibility or incompatibility of the particular religions—will contribute to turning the conflict in a more creative direction.

Note Number Five: Dancing in the Divine Presence and the Study of Ritual

Western scholars of religion, especially those who come out of Protestant Christianity, have perhaps placed too much emphasis on "belief" in the study of religion. When one moves outside the Western traditions—but even here the importance of ritual needs to be more fully acknowledged—one quickly encounters the centrality of ritual or dancing in the presence of God to many traditions. The centrality of rituals, festivals, or gestures of the holy is reflected in the very calendars of the non-Western world. I learned recently that the traditional calendar of Bali, for example, is basically for the purpose of indicating the timing of rituals that permeate the society of Bali throughout the lunar year. And here in India one encounters an astonishing number of festivals in the Hindu community, and rarely a day could be found on which some festival is not celebrated in some part of the country. Indeed in some of the bhakti or devotional traditions, festival, dance, ritual, and pilgrimage are the chief expressions of a life of devotion. Here participation takes precedence over the other notes of the religious life: it is being caught up in the life of the Divine as it is acted out, performed, not in the sense of artificiality, but as itr is lived, that is crucial.

The bias of Western scholarship towards belief is reflected in the volume after volume on the doctrine of this or that tradition that appears in comparison to the much smaller number of studies on the ritual life and expressions of the different traditions. We in the study of religion need, I believe, to give more attention to the religious experience of ritual as an expression of living in the presence of the Divine.

Note Number Six: Remembering the Whence, the Historical Dimension

Even though I have emphasized the living encounter of men and women of different faiths as our point of departure, I do not mean, nor do I think it possible, to underestimate the importance of historical study. Every religious person has a whence, both a source in the historical flow of things and a place in the unfolding of generations. Thus we are led to understand that history that provides the backdrop to the present. But I cannot agree with Professor Ninian Smart that placing religion in a historical perspective is the great achievement of the modern study of religion.[10] Here we must recognize the limitations of the historical method, not only the tendency to historicism but also that many religions do not understand themselves in historical terms. Thus to insist on this frame of interpretation may be inadequate and distort their own self-understanding. Nevertheless, it does seem that persons in every tradition have a sense of their whence: the guru and guru's guru that initiates, the lineage of one's teachers, and the traditions of one's sacred texts are all ways of situating oneself in relation to those who came before. And it is this story that is remembered in the lives of religious persons and of believing communities. Thus the scholar of religion is obliged also to pay attention to the historical as the living backdrop to the present generation's experience of the tradition. Historical scholarship can also be disturbing to the religious community as it always makes one aware of both the elements of continuity and discontinuity within the tradition. Let me quickly mention two further notes in this new key.

Note Number Seven: Communities of Faith Living the Melody

Religious life is not only embodied in persons and traditions, but also in communities of faith that must themselves harmonize in the distinctive ways of living the melody found in each tradition. Within every community of faith are to be found those who live the melody in more ritualistic ways, those who live it in more mystical ways, those who live it in more moral (and moralist) ways, those who live it in more intellectual ways, etc. This internal variety contributes to the richness of a community's life, but it also creates tension as there is a continual internal conversation in every community about the best way to live the melody. This multiplicity of types within each community of faith is also the basis for the recognition of commonalities across traditions, commonalities that involve mystics in different traditions, moralists in different traditions, intellectuals in different traditions, etc. But here again we encounter the dialectic of same yet different, different yet similar.

While, for example, the Sufi, the Sant, the Pir, the Ricchi, and the Saint may all be mystics, their internal experience has been shaped and articulated by the distinctive paths that have nurtured them. Thus we must respect both the differences and the points of contact, and perhaps their common witness to a Beyond in which they are caught up and transformed. My point, once again, is one of caution, of comparative study preceding only on the basis of rigorous fidelity to the lives, texts, traditions, and communities we are seeking to understand.

Note Number Eight: The Unfinshed Symphony: The Future of Religious Pathways

Finally, the student of religion must be aware that the traditions of faith are still unfinished, still in process, still unfolding, still between the Beyond from which they emerged and towards which they go. Likewise, the relations between the different traditions remain in process and will not be settled by the works of scholarship. Whether or not these many melodies will contribute to an even greater symphony we cannot know. But yet the scholar of religion has a worthy vocation: to contribute to understanding, both within and between traditions, of the religious heritage and living present of the religious story of humankind.[11]

That story is as infinitely varied as the millions of human beings who today live out the present chapter, as multiform as the different pathways of traditions that seek to lead us to the Beyond, and yet as unitary as the story of humankind in relation to that Beyond which has been heard singing the many melodies of the Ultimate. The end of it all we may not know, nor need we. What should suffice for the scholar of religion is the opportunity to attempt to understand, to hear something of the music amidst all the dissonance. And if I am right then that means that she must cultivate an ear for the Mystery of the Beyond, a disciplined imagination that will allow her to walk with another, remembering the priority of the human face we wish to understand, aware of the manifold pathways of the religious life and their manifold dimensions, and with a sensitivity to the dancing forms that come before us. Such a scholar will not forsake the demands of fidelity in depth for superficial similarities, or be content to offer superficial explanations when deeper understanding is called for. They will, in the words of the Quran, "follow that which is inspired in thee from the Lord" (Surah 33.2).

Taken together these "notes" would lead to a "new key" in the study of religion. A key to be sung in different ways according to the improvisation of the singer/scholar and in harmony with the divine melody one encounters in the study of the pathways to the Beyond, pathways that unfold in response to the cosmic harmony it is our gift to receive.

Endnotes

[1] S. H. Vahiddudin, *Religion at the Crossroads* (Delhi: Idarah-i Adabiyat-i Delli, 1980), 8.

[2] Ninian Smart, *Beyond Ideology* (New York: Harper & Row, 1981), 54.

[3] I have suggested some of those "masters" above. I might also mention John Blofeld and his studies of the Taoist tradition and

J. V. Murti and his studies of Buddhism.

[4] Wilfred Cantwell Smith, "Comparative Religion: Whither and Why?" in *The History of Religions: Essays in Methodology*, ed. Mircea Eliade and J. M. Kitagawa (Chicago: University of Chicago Press, 1959), 52.

[5] Gandhi, *Harijan*, 22 September, 1946.

[6] Margaret Chatterjee, *Gandhi's Religious Thought* (London: Macmillan Press, 1983).

[7] Gandhi, *The Story of My Experiments with Truth*, 1st ed. (Ahmedabad: Narajivan Press, 1927).

[8] For a fuller discussion of the grammatical or cruciform method indicated here see Eugen Rosenstock-Huessy, *Speech and Reality* (Norwich VT: Argo Books, 1973) and M. D. Bryant and Hans Huessy, ed., *Eugen Rosenstock Huessy: Studies in His Life and Thought* (Lewiston, NY: The Edwin Mellen Press, 1986).

[9] See the study at the Indian Institute of Islamic Studies in New Delhi entitled "Inter-Religious Perceptions of Hindus and Muslims," 1982.

[10] Smart, *Beyond Ideology*, 24 ff.

[11] Since I gave these lectures, I have written a volume which contributes to the last note mentioned here. It is entitled *Woven on the Loom of Time: Many Faiths and One Divine Purpose* (New Delhi: Suryodaya/Decent Books, 1999).

Shinto Shrine in Kyoto, Japan

PART II

Three Essays In the Dialogue of Religions

IV
Inter-Religious Dialogue: The Problems and Prospects of "Overcoming History"

This essay was first given as a lecture at the Embassy of the Islamic Republic of Iran in New Delhi. Although it addresses the larger issue of "overcoming history" in order that we might begin a new era in the relations between people of different faiths, my main instances are Muslim/Christian and Hindu/Christian. I trust it will contribute to dialogue and understanding between men and women of different faiths.[1]

Let me begin with a few qualifications. First, I must acknowledge that I am not a specialist in Islam, nor of the Hindu traditions. But I am a student of comparative religion and, more importantly, I have come to have some knowledge of the Muslim and Hindu faiths and worlds through my involvement in the dialogue of Muslims, Hindus, Christians, Jews and the peoples of diverse faiths. It is in this context that I have developed some living awareness of the power of faith in Allah, the acknowledgement of Mohammad as his prophet, and of the manifold ways to the Absolute found in the Hindu traditions. Second, I must admit that I do not know either Arabic or Sanskrit. Thus I have not been able to recite the Qu'ran in its proper language but only in translation. Likewise, Hindu scriptures are only known to me in translation. Third, I must acknowledge that as well as being a student of the religious life of humankind I am also a Christian. I say this in order that you understand the tradition that has shaped me.

In the contemporary dialogue of people of different faiths there is no wholly neutral standpoint, for all of us bring to that dialogue the particular faiths that have shaped us. And each of us are part of one or another of the varied traditions of faith and culture. Thus no one is priviledged, no one stands outside, no one occupies a neutral standpoint.

Fourth, and finally, I must acknowledge with gratitude the opportunity to spend part of an earlier sabbatical in the Indian Institute of Islamic Studies. Dr. Syed Ausaf Ali, its founder, has helped me to understand something of the tradition of Islam. I suppose that one of the first things that often surprises a Western student of religion is to discover that Islam is not confined to the Arab peoples but embraces diverse racial and ethnic communities, from Indonesia to India and the former Soviet Union, from Iran through the Middle East and down into Africa. It is also worth noting that Islam is now the fastest growing religious community in both the USA and Canada. (Some within the black community in the USA see it as an "empowering Way" without the racism of American Christianity.) And during that same sabbatical year I was also a visiting scholar at the Radhakrishnan Institute for Advanced Studies in Philosophy at the University of Madras and was initiated into the world of devotion to Lord Krishna at Vrindaban through my good friend, Sri Shrivatsa Goswami. I mention these things because it is part of the thesis of this essay that we will only begin to "overcome history" as we begin to create a new history of relationships between persons of the different traditions.[2]

But let me now turn to the essay proper and place over it two verses, one from the Qu'ran and one from the Upanishads. First, from the Qu'ran:

[In A. Yusaf Ali's translation] Let there be no compulsion in religion. Truth stands out clear from error: whoever rejects evil and believes in God hath grasped the most trustworthy handhold, that never breaks ... (Surah 2:256).[3]

Taj Mahal in Agra, India

Second, from the Isa Upanishad:

[In Juan Mascaro's translation] Behold the universe in the glory of God: and all that lives and moves on earth. Leaving the transient, find joy in the Eternal: set not your heart on another's possession."[4]

We shall return to these quotations at the end of the essay, but for now just let them stand without comment.

Here I intend to do four things: (1) to unfold something of the history that must be overcome, (2) to point to a way of meeting between different faiths, (3) to highlight some of the outstanding issues that Hindus, Christians, and Muslims must address, and (4) to conclude with some recommendations.[5]

On Overcoming History: A Clarification

I have entitled this essay on interreligious dialogue "Overcoming History" for the simple reason that in order for there to be a significant encounter and dialogue between men and women of different faiths it will be necessary to overcome the long history of antagonism between the different traditions. Let me illustrate this in relation to Muslim/Christian relations. Perhaps in no instance is our thesis as painfully obvious as it is in relation to these two remarkable faiths: Islam and Christianity. In his introduction to *The Concise Encyclopedia of Islam*, Huston Smith says simply and directly "during most of their history, Muslims and Christians have been at odds...."[6] Albert Hourani, in his *Islam in European Thought* writes, "from the time it first appeared, the religion of Islam was a problem for Christian Europe. Those who believed in it were the enemy on the frontier."[7] Such statements could be multiplied by citing other authorities but these will suffice.

From the very beginning of the Muslim era, Christians, especially in the West, have misunderstood, misrepresented, and maligned the faith of those who regard Mohammad as "the Messenger of God." Albert Hourani characterizes the Christian attitude in this way: "they (Christians) knew that Muslims believed in one God . . . but they could not easily accept that Mohammad was an authentic prophet . . . . The teaching of Mohammad . . . was [perceived as] a denial of the central doctrines of Christianity . . . ."[8] Thus it is essential that the Christian world repent of its failure to adequately acknowledge the faith of Islam. The Christian stereotype of Islam begins with a mistake about its very name. Rather than recognizing Islam for what it is, namely, "the perfect peace which comes from surrender to Allah," for centuries Christians have referred to Islam as "Mohammadanism." This is an error which strikes at the very heart of Islamic faith in Allah. It is only recently that Western Christians have even begun to name aright the great tradition of Islam. The West is just beginning to learn the fundamentals of Islam: the Five Pillars, the Qu'ran, and the prophet Mohammad.[9]

But it is not Christians alone who have failed to grasp the faith of Muslims. If I may be so bold, Muslims have also often characterized the Christian faith in ways that would not be acceptable to authentic Christians. Again let me turn

79

to Albert Hourani: "For Muslim thinkers, the status of Christianity was clear. Jesus was one of the line of authentic prophets which had culminated in Mohammad, the 'Seal of the Prophets,' and his authentic message was essentially the same as that of Mohammad. Christians had misunderstood their faith, however, as they thought of their prophet as god, and believed he had been crucified . . . ."[10] While Muslims have always, in their own terms, recognized Jesus, they have often not been very positive about Christianity.

It is this history, one at once Christian and Muslim, that must be overcome. And, unfortunately, it is this story that in its own distinctive versions and notes is too often with us in the relations between the Abrahamic traditions of Judaism, Christianity, and Islam and the other religious traditions of humankind. As one Hindu commented to a Christian concerning the longer history of Christian relations with the Hindu world "[in] all matters concerning *dharma* you were deadly against us, violently or stealthily." In the relations between the non-Abrahamic traditions, the pattern has often been different when in China Confucian, Taoist, and Buddhist *chiao* or teachings came to accommodate each other in ways that overcame the need for exclusive allegiance.[11]

Both of these patterns have been even more complicated in our century by the emergence of a secularism (in both Western and Communist versions) that regards all religion as superstition (or an *opiate* à la Marx or an *illusion* à la Freud) and a vestige of a past age and not worthy of respect nor understanding.

Let me explain why I began with "history" and the sense in which I am here using the term. In 1993, at the University of Waterloo, I invited a Muslim woman from Waterloo (originally from India) to present to my class on "interreligious encounter and dialogue" something of the faith of Islam. She did a splendid job of outlining the major features of the Islamic faith. But in the discussion that followed, she made the following statement: "Christians have always been hostile to

Islam. Look at what's happening in Bosnia: Christians are killing Muslims and everyone just stands by and watches. It's a continuation of the Crusades." I was shocked by her statement. Partly because I realize that there is some truth to it—it is probably true that many countries in Europe and North America are not as exercised by these events as they would be if Christians were being slaughtered—and that in itself is appalling. But her statement also made me realize that for many (both in the Muslim and Christian world) the "Crusades" is not just an event of medieval history. It continues to be a living sense of the ongoing relationship between Christians and Muslims. While it is perhaps understandable— given the depth of Christian misunderstanding of and antagonism towards Islam—that a Muslim would perceive Christianity as a hostile, aggressive force—it is also disconcerting.

The second story involves Christian responses to the Hindu world. I regularly take my students to visit Muslim Masjids, Sikh Gurdwaras, and Hindu Mandirs, and the more typical Christian comment, often heard from my students when I take them to a Hindu temple, is "yes, but that's all idolatry." It is a comment that just comes spontaneously from their Christian background and does not have anything to do with what the Hindus have just told us about the images we have seen in their mandir or temple. It is often a long and difficult process to get my students to understand the "images of the Absolute" that one encounters in the Hindu traditions *in their own terms*. For Hindus, images of the Absolute are not forbidden. Indeed they are essential. The image gives form to the believers for their sake, but none of the forms are the Absolute itself which is beyond all form. "Nameless and Formless Thou art, O Thou Unknowable. All forms of the universe are Thine: thus Thou art known" is the way it is put in a hymn of praise to the Great Goddess. [12]

What these comments make clear is that we all, whether Christian or Muslim or Hindu come to the encounter and

Jama Masjid in Delhi, India

dialogue between faiths burdened, for good and ill, by the legacy of the past. We are, as Eugen Rosenstock-Huessy saw so clearly, creatures who, while living in the present, face four directions simultaneously.[13] Backward and forward in time, inward and outward in space. And here at the intersection of these four fronts—the crux where we live—we are confronted continuously with what from the past we need to let go of and what we need to retain, what from the future we must respond to and that to which we must say no. These are certainly questions that confront the believers in all traditions in the present situation.

The issue for us is not "overcoming history" in some specialized or professional sense, nor is it a task of rewriting history. Rather, *it is the past that lives in the present and shapes our perceptions and responses to the faith of the other that must be overcome.*

I will not presume to say what that past might be in Muslim and Hindu consciousness, but let me illustrate this by making some points about the Christian world in the USA and Canada.

The images of Islam especially in the contemporary West are not positive. Some of the images North Americans have of Muslims are that Muslims are people who attempt to blow up the World Trade Centre in New York City. (And now, after September 11, 2001, they are fanatics who hijack airplanes and slam them into the WTC killing thousands.) They are terrorists in the Middle East or oil-rich Sheiks who live without regard for the everyday Muslim in their home country. They have no regard for the rights of women. They are led by fanatical leaders in North Africa and the Middle East. And I could go on and on. Writing in 1983, R. Marston Speight in *Christian-Muslim Relations*, wrote,

> In general . . . the people of this country remain uninformed as to what Islam is and what Muslims are like . . . the prejudices and stereotypes of the past still persist so that the image projected of Islam upon the imagination of the average American is one of intolerant, legalistic, and fatalistic religion . . . .[14]

Little seems to change.

And the story is not that positive in relation to images of Hindus among Christians. Hindus have long been regarded by Christians in North America as primitive, poor, and pagan. They should be the object of Christian charity and missionary work. In recent decades the view began to shift as we regarded Hindus as tolerant but that image has been tarnished by the Ayodhya affair.[15] Most people in North America probably still regard Hindus as impoverished snake charmers and "idolaters." These attitudes continue down into the present.[16]

Occasionally a voice does challenge these prejudices about people of other faiths. On September 14, 1993, former U.S. President Jimmy Carter (a devout Christian) commented on the American attitude towards the Muslim world in *The Times of India*, saying: "I think there is too much of an inclination in this country to look on Muslims as inherently terrorist or inherently against the West." I was very pleased to see this statement, and it needs to be made often in the current climate in North America.

Let me be very clear. I am not saying that any of these negative images are correct. But I am saying that they are the ones that dominate the public media and the public consciousness of Christians (and the secular or non-religious as well) in the USA and Canada. And they are all negative. They do not serve the cause of truth and understanding between people of different faiths but they do serve the cause of secular political and religious forces that would maintain the long legacy of bitter relations between communities of different faiths. Thus both the contemporary situation and the historical record do not bode well for any significant encounter and dialogue between people of diverse faiths.

On the Possibility of Encounter and Dialogue

Are we doomed to endlessly repeat history? Is there an inherent hostility, as someone recently said to me, between religions? Is there a way to overcome this past and move towards a new day in the relations between people of different faiths? I believe that there is, and that is the way of interfaith encounter and dialogue.[17] This movement heralds a new day for relations between different faiths and faith communities. It has as its aim mutual understanding and mutual recognition. Just as the past and present history of bitter relations between people of different faiths is the consequence of human acts that promoted antagonism and hatred against those they did not know for motives that were dark and ignorant, so a new history can grow out of the acts of understanding, compassion, and mutuality that are the fruit of dialogue.

In a meeting of faiths characterized by dialogue, it is essential that each community be *allowed to define itself*. This is the first rule of dialogue. Rather than insisting on our perception of the other, we must begin with the other's understanding of its own faith and community. When Hindus, Christians, Buddhists, Sikhs, Confucianists and Muslims (to name but a few) meet in this way, then we can move beyond the stereotypes and misperceptions of the past and be open to the other in terms of its own self-understanding, its own faith. When people of different faiths begin to truly meet, we will begin to confront the living past and we will experience some of the dissonance between our preconceptions and prejudices and the reality of the other faith. I remember with considerable embarrassment my own encounters with Muslims and Hindus over the past twenty years. I recognize that I too was caught in some of the prejudices and misconceptions I mentioned earlier. I was so surprised to meet Indian and Indonesian and Saudi Muslims who did not fit my expectations. And I discovered that Hindu devotion was often deeper and more profound than found in my own community of faith and that they were not all "idolaters." Through meeting in the spirit of dialogue, then, I had to confront my own "living past" and "overcome" it so that I might relate to the reality of the other.

In the encounter and dialogue between people of different faiths, the obligation is to listen to the other and attempt to understand them *in their own terms*, and to relate to them in accordance with their own self-understanding and vice-versa. This approach overcomes the too familiar pattern of either assuming one knows the faith of the other, or attempting to force them into the stereotypes of the past. Nowhere perhaps is this more obvious then the way we in the Abrahamic traditions regard the images of the Divine that are so present in Hindu life and culture. Rather than seeing them in our terms and its assumptions we need to see them in terms of the assumptions and religious contexts of those for whom they are "images of the Divine."[18] We need to meet in a freshness and openness of spirit, willing to allow ourselves to be surprised and moved by the *din*/faith in Allah and His Prophet Mohammad, or by the faith in Jesus as the Christ, or by devotion to Krishna and Radha. This is the second rule of dialogue.

The third rule of dialogue is that when we meet in dialogue, we meet as fellow human beings and pilgrims in faith. Too often in the history of religion we have "demonized" those of other faiths. We in the Christian traditions have too often called all non-Christians "pagans" and acted as if God were not present to other peoples unless we Christians were there. This is an insufferable arrogance and a betrayal of faith in the God who is the Creator, Redeemer, and Sanctifier of humankind. There are parallels to this attitude in other religions. However, when we meet in dialogue, we quickly discover that we share a common humanity (although some follow the Christian way of being human, others the Muslim way of being human, others the Hindu ways, others the Buddhist way, and so on) and that we are fellow pilgrims in our respective journeys towards the Absolute. We do not have the same faith; we have our own distinctive faiths. But at the same time, we discover crucial things that are shared across tradition: beliefs in the Ultimate, values of compassion and virtue, concerns for the welfare of "all sentient beings" (as the Buddhists say), an antipathy to evil and so on. To come into dialogue and to recognize these shared values is illuminating and transforming. It can and will profoundly alter the relations between the faith communities.

A similar point has been made by Klaus Klostermaier in writing about Hindu-Christian dialogue,

> Dialogue is primarily the meeting between human beings. Hindu-Christian dialogue is not so much the meeting between Hinduism and Christianity as between Hindus and Christians, each professing his (or her) own faith. Dialogue stems . . . from a profound recognition of the mutuality of our common life . . . it deepens our sensitivity and promotes understanding . . ."[19]

The fourth rule of dialogue—and the last one I will mention here—is that in the meeting of people of different faiths, it is essential that the depths of the respective faiths come to expression. There is often a misconception of what occurs in dialogue. Many believe that it is a polite meeting where the depths of our respective faiths are set aside in the name of an easy tolerance. But this is a misconception. Genuine encounter and dialogue is a meeting of the deepest levels of our respective faiths, where we bear witness to what of the spirit and of the Absolute has been given to us. This we do not for the sake of persuading the other that we are right and they are wrong, but for the sake of bearing witness to what each has experienced and knows of the One who is beyond. When we meet in this way, when the dialogue goes this deeply, then all involved can grow not only in their own faith but in their recognition of the validity of the other.

We will sometimes encounter profound differences that we cannot accept. But even here we must be willing to let those differences stand as we continue our efforts to appreciate the other faith. Klaus Klostermaier puts it this way,

> the encounter of two absolute Truth claims . . . does not end with an abandoning of the absolute Truth claim on either side or on both sides, nor does it result in quarrels in order to establish one truth claim against the other, nor is just politely keeping silent in order not to offend the other partner, knowing well that he or she must be wrong . . . . Hindu-Christian dialogue goes on and brings both partners to realise the limits and values of their own 'truths' in their traditions and it constantly kindles the spark of the *pneuma*; it renews the *eros*, gives greater emphasis to the *mumuksutvam*; it makes the partner more open for Truth— and that is how we come nearer to Truth."[20]

Sometimes, however, we will discover that differences do not always threaten, but can be the occasion for profound intellectual, moral, or spiritual growth.

A similar point was made by John Taylor and Muzammil Siddiqi in "Understanding and Experience of Christian-Muslim Dialogue" when they wrote:

Dialogue was essentially to be undertaken in a spirit of repentance wherein we turned our backs on past and present prejudice, wherein we turned to our neighbor in the spirit of love, wherein we turned to God, as He offered Himself to us."[21]

Through meeting in a spirit of dialogue — taking the other seriously on its own terms, listening profoundly and speaking truthfully, growing in appreciation of our shared humanity across tradition, and witnessing to the Ultimate who is the source and object of genuine faith — we can begin to overcome history and enter a new day in the relations between faiths. Fortunately, this is not merely a theoretical or "Pollyanna" statement since there are already pioneers of the dialogue between religions that have begun to build new understanding and different relations between traditions of faith. I think here of Swami Abhishiktananda/Henri LeSaux, Bede Griffiths and Vandana Mataji as Christians in dialogue with Hindus at a profound level, or Swami Chidananda and Swami Ranganathananda for their encounter with Christianity or of Dr. Shivacharya Shivamurthy for his efforts to build Hindu-Muslim understanding in Karnataka and for Syed Ausaf Ali, who has championed dialogue between Muslims and people of other faiths for more than three decades. In these people and many others that new history is beginning to dawn.[22]

Can We Value the Faith of the Other?

As I have already indicated, the first problem to be overcome is the appalling ignorance of the West concerning other faiths, but especially Islam. This can be achieved most powerfully and profoundly through face-to-face meetings of Christians and Muslims. In such meetings, stereotypes and misconceptions quickly give way to an acknowledgement of the integrity and depth of each other's faith and path. The same can be said for the meeting of Hindus and Christians. The second way is through education. We need to include education about the many religious traditions of humankind in our schools. Such education should not serve the apologetic interests of a given religious community, but should be an account of the various faiths that a believer in a given tradition can recognize as valid. I say this because I believe it essential that the study of religion be not only accurate and historically sound, but also convey something of the living heart of the various traditions.[23] Such education about the different religious traditions should also be a critical education, that is, it should not fail to speak accurately and critically of the way in which each tradition has lived its faith or has failed to live its faith in history.

The legacy of ignorance and antagonism between the religious traditions will not be overcome without inspired religious leadership. Those in positions of authority within their respective communities of faith must take up the cause of respecting other faiths and seek to communicate that respect for other Ways to their own communities. No one, to my mind, has done this more profoundly in our time than H. H. the Dalai Lama. One repeatedly finds in his writings and his speeches positive statements about other faiths. Let me quote him speaking to his own community:

> We should accept that there are many different religions and that each one is valuable. Each religion has a special technique and message for humanity ... despite having different philosophies, all religions teach us to be good human beings . . . all religions have the potential to produce good human beings. [24]

Think of the impact such words would have if spoken by all religious leaders.

When we meet one another on the basis of mutual respect and some understanding of the faith of the other, then there will be other issues we must address. There will be complex theological issues to address: our understandings of the Divine, our differing understandings of Jesus/Isa, our differing views of the Qu'ran, Bible, Vedas, and other scriptures, etc. Among other issues are two that I would highlight as crucial for consideration: fundamentalism and conversionism. I have stated them in this way deliberately, for I want you to understand each for what it is—namely, an "ideology," as indicated by the suffix "ism." Let me try to make this clearer.

Fundamentalism

One of the problems that faces many communities of faith is that of "fundamentalism." I know that many within the Muslim world do not like to use this term, since they rightly see it as having originated in the Christian world and as first defining a Christian phenomenon. And it is a term that some Hindus reject because it distorts what they consider to be a legitimate affirmation of their own Hindu way. But if we can move beyond these polemics to the reality, then we can see the issue. If the movement we call "fundamentalism" is a return to the fundamentals of faith, then *it is legitimate,* for it revitalizes the faith of the community. But this is not what the term usually connotes. The "fundamentalism" that must concern all communities is when faith is transformed into a closed ideology. The ideology then becomes a way to clothe or mask the fear and alienated consciousness of a group. The living faith of Hindus then becomes the ideology of "Hindutva" that leaves no place for people of other faiths, or the living "din" of Muslims becomes the ideology of "Jihad" that perceives everyone else as an enemy, or the living faith of Christians becomes the iron clad ideology that sees those outside the fold as not only enemies but "damned."

Studies of Christian fundamentalism in the United States have shown that fundamentalism arises among sectors of the Christian population that have been marginalized and feel threatened by modern conditions of life and advances in knowledge. They react by articulating an ideological version of the Christian faith—inerrant scripture, insistence on certain dogmatic formulas, opposition to modern life, etc.—that is not open to question, but must simply be affirmed in the ideological terms of the group. This reaction and development can be found across many religious communities, and it needs to be addressed from within our respective religious communities. Such an ideology does not lead to a vital faith in Allah or God or the Absolute , but rather legitimizes the fears of the group. When, in the name of Hinduism or Islam or Christianity, one proclaims "death" to those whose faith is different from yours, this is not authentic Hinduism, nor authentic Islam nor authentic Christianity.[25]

Conversionism

Another issue, especially of the Christian world, that must be addressed if we are to move towards dialogical mutuality and understanding is "conversionism." I mean here the attitude that the only way to relate to people of other faiths—Buddhist, Muslim, Hindu, Confucian, or non-believer—is to seek their conversion. This assumption is based on a profound confusion. In the Christian faith, *metanoia* or conversion is what follows in response to hearing the command to "Follow Me." Thus it is a word directed towards the disciple, the follower, the Christian. It is the Christian who is called to "be turned around" to be "renewed in mind and spirit" which is the meaning of conversion. But far too often, Christians project this need onto someone else, the Other, whether Muslim or Hindu or Jew or Buddhist or even fellow Christian, rather than seeing it as their own deepest need. Parallel attitudes are to be found within the Muslim world and even in the tolerant world of Hinduism. But the point is that such a mentality stands in the way of dialogue, in the way of authentic meeting where Muslim and Christian and Hindu meet one another as brothers and sisters seeking to understand the One who is gracious and beneficent and beyond. It is not an issue of qualifying the Truth that has been given to us in our respective traditions, but of not insisting that our Truth exhausts all Truth.

It would be better for Christians to follow the lead of Vatican II which said:

the church also regards with esteem the Muslims who worship the One, Subsistent, Merciful, and Almighty God, the Creator of Heaven and earth, who has spoken to man ... to make sincere efforts at mutual understanding and to work together ... [26]

Can we move in this direction?

These are but some of the issues that will need to be addressed in the encounter and dialogue between people of different faiths. From this dialogue there will not always emerge agreement; but even in our differences, we will have a deeper understanding of one another.

A Final Word

If there is to be a future of dialogue between different faiths, then it will be necessary to overcome the bitter legacy of the past and present.

Caricatures and stereotypes of each other must give way to accurate understanding and mutual respect. This can only happen as we learn about each other, meet one another, study one another's faith and history, and seek to grasp our respective structures of belief and practice. It is imperative, for example, for the non-Muslim world to understand, as R. Zakaria has written, that "The Prophet is presented in the Qu'ran as the best example of its teachings and a perfect model of human behaviour."[27] Just as it is imperative for Muslims to understand that when Christians affirm that Jesus is the Christ, they do not diminish the God who is One. And we in the Abrahamic faiths must learn that the Hindu ways to the Absolute are not necessarily a rejection of the One God.

We will also have to come to understand that there is diversity within each tradition. While Christians from East and West share a common faith, they are also diverse not only in terms of Orthodox, Catholic, and Protestant, but also in terms of different cultural and ethnic settings. Likewise, in Islam there are Shiites and Sunnis, and just as Muslims from West and East share the faith of Islam, they live it in different and changing ways across the Muslim world. Studies in Islam in the Indian, Indonesian, and Central Asian contexts—as well as Iranian and Nigerian—are making us all aware of the plurality within Islam itself. The problem is different as we move closer to the Hindu world where we will have to learn to see the unity across the diversity of communities and ways in the Hindu world.[28]

As we begin to encounter and dialogue with one another, then the prejudices and misconceptions that have entered our respective cultures and literatures will begin to be overcome. We need to reach a day when Muslims understand aright Christian and Hindu texts and Christians understand aright the Qu'ran and other writings of Muslims and those of the Hindus, and Hindus understand the texts of Christians and Muslims. We should all have the experience I have had reading the works of people such as the late Dr. Krishna Sivaraman the great Saivite scholar who worked most of his life in Canada or the remarkable Sufi scholar from Iran, Dr. Hossein Nasr, or Abdullah Durkee and many other Muslim and Hindu writers: the experience of growing in understanding of and sympathy with the other faith.[29]

At the outset, I placed two verses over this essay, one from the Qu'ran and one from the Upanishads. Please forgive my audacity in offering these comments on them. The first, I believe, states a truth that Hindus, Muslims and Christians should affirm, namely, that in matters of religion there should be "no compulsion." Instead, we need to respect all those who "reject evil" and "believe in God" since this is the "most dependable handle." But it is important to link this Qu'ranic verse with the second verse from the Upanishads which urges all to "behold the universe in the Glory of God." This again I understand globally, as wisdom for believers in all traditions. For it is in beholding all—and that includes all the religious ways of humankind—in the "glory of God" that we find "joy" and do not set our hearts on "another's possession." For it is important to understand that in the dialogue between religions, we are called not to reduce the intensity or depth of our own faith but to bear witness to it while respecting the faith of the other. So the proper contest between believers is not, I believe, in terms of the superiority of my faith over yours, but in the depth of our devotion to the One that Muslims call Allah, that Christians call God, and that Hindus call by many Names. For it is that One and that One alone who should be the object of our striving and our faith.[30]

Endnotes

[1] A lecture given at the Embassay of the Islamic Republic of Iran, October 27, 1993. It is partly based on a lecture given at the Center of Advanced Study in History at Aligarh Muslim University, Aligarh, India, in September 1993. I have made a few corrections/additions, but I have resisted making the many additions that could be made following September 11, 2001. These events only deepen, in my view, the need for encounter and dialogue.

[2] Some of the consequences of my experience and research during that year are found in this volume.

[3] A. Yusaf Ali, Qu'ran, Surah 2:256. Compare the translation by R. Zakaria, *Muhammad and the* Quran (New Delhi: Penguin Books, India, 1991), 105.

[4] Juan Mascaro, trans., *The Upanishads* (London: Penguin Books, 1988), 49.

[5] The more specific theological points of convergence and conflict between Islam, Hinduism and Christianity will not be addressed here; that would require several further essays.

[6] Huston Smith, introduction to *The Concise Encyclopedia of Islam*, ed. C. Glasse (London: Stacey International), 5. In this context it is also worth noting Smith's citation of Meg Greenfield writing in *Newsweek* in 1979, "We are heading into an expansion of that complex religion, culture, and geography known as Islam. There are two things to be said about this. One is that no part of the world is more important . . . for the foreseeable future. The other is that no part of the world is more hopelessly and systematically and stubbornly misunderstood by us."

[7] Albert Hourani, *Islam in European Thought* (Cambridge:

Cambridge University Press, 1991), 6.

[8] *Ibid.*, 8. Another Christian attitude towards Islam, and one more acceptable, is that found in the writings of now Bishop Kenneth Cragg, beginning with *The Call of the Mineret* in 1957. Occasionally there was a glimmer of another view as when Pope Gregory VII wrote to Prince al-nasir in 1076, "there is a charity which we owe to each other more than the other peoples because we recognize and confess one sole God, although in different ways..." cited in Hourani, 9.

[9] There are now several good introductions to Islam available in the West. One of the most accessible and readable is Huston Smith, *The World's Religions* (San Francisco: Harper and Row, 1991).

[10] Hourani, 8. This is again not simply a medieval attitude, it is still present in volumes like *Islam and Christianity* (Istanbul: Waqf Ikhlas Publications No. 12, 1991).

[11] Sivendra Prakash in C.M. Rogers and Sivendra Prakash, "Hindu-Christian Dialogue Postponed," in *Dialogue Between Men of Living Faiths*, ed. S. J. Samantha (Geneva: WCC, 1971). For the larger discussion see G. Parrinder, gen. ed., *Man And His Gods: Encyclopedia of the World's Religions* (London: Hamlyn, 1974), especially W.A.C.H. Dobson's "China," 263-306; Arnold Toynbee, *An Historian's Approach to Religion* (London: Oxford University Press, 1956); W. E. Hocking, *The Coming World Civilization* (New York: Harper & Brothers, 1956), especially "Guides of Interaction among Universal Religions," 110ff.; and Hajime Nakamura, *A Comparative History of Ideas* (Delhi: Motilal Banarsidass, 1992).

[12] See Diana Eck, *Darsan: Seeing the Divine Image in India* (Chambersburg, PA: Anima Books, 1985). She cites Mark Twain who visited Banaras in the 1890s and wrote, "Idols. What a swarm of them there is! The town is a vast museum of idols—and all of them crude, misshapen, and ugly." (18). This ignorance is still too much with us. The quotation in praise of the Great Goddess is found on p. 28. See also Arun Shourie, *Hinduism: Essence and Consequence* (Sahibabad: Vikas Publishing House, 1979), especially the chapter entitled "One End, Many Means," 92ff. He argues that "Just as there is only one reality, there is only one aim for man: to perceive that reality, to dissolve in it, to be one with Brahman" (92). And later, he says, ". . . the Upanishads teach us, realizing the Brahman and, upon realization, dissolving in Him,

is the only aim or man" (96).

[13] See Eugen Rosenstock-Huessy, *Speech and Reality* (Norwich, VT: Argo Books, 1968). For an introduction to this remarkable but little known thinker see M. Darrol Bryant and Hans Huessy, *Eugen Rosenstock-Huessy: Studies in his Life and Thought* (Lewiston, NY: Edwin Mellem Press, 1985).

[14] R. Marston Speight, *Christian-Muslim Relations, An Introduction for Christians in the USA* (Hartford, CN: NCCUSA, 1983), 2.

[15] See Asghar A. Engineer, ed., *Babri Masjid Ramjanambhomi Controversy*, (Delhi: Ajanta Publications, 1990). The editor remarks that this is ". . . one of the major controversies which has been exploited politically . . . in post-independence India" (l). See also the fine statement by Dr. Shivamurthy Shivacharya Mahaswamiji, *Communal Conflicts in India*, (Sirigere: Sri Taralabalu Jagadguru Brihanmath, 1993), where he concludes "the need of the hour is not to construct or demolish the Masjid or Mandir. Instead, we should aim at demolishing the walls of hatred and enmity in the minds of Hindus and Muslims and learn to live in harmony as brothers and sisters of the same human family . . ." (36).

[16] See, for example, Eck, *Darsan*, esp. 18ff.

[17] For some of my own contributions to this movement see M. Darrol Bryant & Frank Flinn, eds., *Interreligious Dialogue: Voices from a New Frontier* (New York: Paragon House, 1985), and chapter 2 of this volume. See also Herbert Jai Singh, ed., *Inter-Religious Dialogue* (Bangalore: Christian Institute for the Study of Religion and Society, 1967).

[18] In the foreword to Diana Eck's *Darsan*, we read ". . . it is our worldview, our philosophy, which prevents us from seriously considering the Hindu claim that Siva and Krishna, and their images, truly contain or manifest the divine . . . . So far from seeing ugly idols, we would then see with a vision which includes and advances understanding" (ii).

[19] Klaus Klostermaier, "Hindu-Christian Dialogue," in S.J. Samartha, *Dialogue Between Men of Living Faiths*, 20. Sivendra Prakash, who is quoted above, continues his comment indicating why many Hindus are now suspicious of the motives of Christians interested in dialogue: ". . . the pity was that your attacks and derogatory remarks were founded in sheer ignorance of what really we are, . . . believe and worship" (22).

[20] Klaus Klostermaier, "A Hindu-Christian Dialogue on Truth" in *Man's Religious Quest*, ed. Whitfield Foy (New York: St. Martin's Press, 1978), 697.

[21] J. Taylor and M. Siddiqi, "Understanding and Experience of Christian-Muslim Dialogue," in S. J. Samartha, *Dialogue*, 60. See also S.J. Samartha & J.B. Taylor, *Christian-Muslim Dialogue* (Geneva: WCC, 1973) and Ismail Raji al-Faruqi, ed., *Trialogue of the Abrahamic Faiths* (International Institute of Islamic Thought, 1982). It should be clear that the call for dialogue is not equivalent to the comparative study of religion or history of religion, though the research and publication of historians of religion and comparativists have certainly contributed to understanding across tradition.

[22] The literature of the dialogical encounter of people of different faiths is beginning to grow dramatically in recent years. Among those writings I will cite just a few: Swami Abishiktananda, *Arunachala: A Christian on Shiva's Mountain* (Delhi: ISPCK, 1982); Vandana, *Gurus, Ashrams, and Christians* (Delhi: ISPCK, 1978), especially Part II on The Guru and the Ashram; and Swami Ranganathananda, *The Christ We Adore* (Calcutta: Advaita Ashrama, 1991). Orbis Books in the USA has established an excellent Faith Meets Faith series.

[23] I should mention here the many contributions of Wilfrid Cantwell Smith to the understanding of Islam, including his *On Understanding Islam* (Delhi: Idarah-i Adabiyat-i Delhi, 1981). For Professor Smith, "to be a Muslim is to participate in the Islamic process in human history . . ." (229). Here Smith emphasizes his role as a student of comparative religion, but he combines this with his Christian commitments in his important, *Towards a World Theology*, in the mid-1980s.

[24] See the Interview with H. H. the Dalai Lama in *Mandala* 13 (October, 1993). This is just one of innumerable examples that could be cited from his writings and his interviews.

[25] There are now many studies appearing on "Fundamentalism." Some are good, others are based on an antipathy to all religion and see every expression of religious fervor or depth as "fundamentalism." Such studies are to be avoided for their anti-religious bias. More useful studies are James Barr, *Fundamentalism* (Philadelphia: Westminster Press, 1978) and Jeffery Hadden and W. Garrett, eds., *Prophetic Religion*, 2 vols.

(New York: Paragon Press, 1986). The major project on "Fundamentalism" under the editorial direction of Martin E. Marty and R. Scott Appleby employs, in my view, a too amorphous definition of the phenomenon, but contains some valuable studies. See their *The Glory and the Power: The Fundamentalist Challenge to the Modern World* (Boston: Beacon Press, 1992), 7ff. and also the three volumes edited by Marty and Appleby, *Fundamentalisms Observed, Fundamentalisms and the State,* and *Fundamentalisms and Society* (Chicago: University of Chicago, 1991 and 1993).

[26] This text is cited in W.M. Watt, *Muslim-Christian Encounter* (London: Routledge, 1991), 148-49. The II Vatican Council statement is cited for the simple reason that it reflects a new departure in the institutional life of the Christian tradition, not because it is fully adequate to what is being called for here.

[27] Zakaria, *Muhammad and the* Quran, 8. For example, Muhammad Ata ur-Rahim's, *Jesus, Prophet of Islam* (Norfolk, UK: Diwan Press, 1977), is not helpful in Christian-Muslim relations. It only takes seriously some hints in the Qu'ran and not the Quranic affirmations of Christians as a "people of the Book." And while it is necessary for Islam to understand its own understanding of Isa/Jesus as a prophet, it is not appropriate to conclude that any other understanding is wrong. Especially since, in dialogue with Christians, it is essential to allow Christians to explain their own faith and not to tell them what they should or should not believe. Nor is Ram Swarup, *Hinduism vis-a-vis Christianity and Islam,* 3d ed. (New Delhi: Voice of India, 1992). While Swarup is right to critique Christian attitudes and practices towards Hindus, he ends up caricaturing Christianity and Islam. He finally says of all Christian theology that it ". . . derives from a mind prejudiced, self-centred and self-righteous. . . [and] above all, like Islam, it is inwoven with bigotry and fanaticism and lacks charity . . ." (63). Since I gave this lecture I have published with S. A. Ali, *Muslim Christian Dialogue: Promise and Problems* (St. Paul: Paragon Press, 1998). I have also published with Christopher Lamb a volume on conversion entitled *Religious Conversion: Contemporary Practices and Controversies* (London: Cassell, 1999).

[28] See William R. Roff, ed., *Islam and the Political Economy of Meaning* (London: Croom Helm, 1987) for a study that contributes to our understanding of Islam in diverse cultural settings. See

also I.Q. Siddiqi, *Islam and Muslims in South Asia: Historical Perspective* (Delhi: Adam Publishers, 1987) and A.F. Imam Ali, *Hindu-Muslim Community in Bangladesh* (Delhi: Kanishka Publication House, 1992). For a discussion of the many communities within the Hindu world see J.R. Hinnells and E.J. Sharpe, *Hinduism* (Newcastle,UK: Oriel Press, 1972).

[29] See, for example, Krishna Sivaraman, *Saivism in Philosophical Perspective* (Delhi: Motilal Banarsidas, 1973), S.H. Nasr, *Knowledge and the Sacred* (Edinburgh: Edinburgh University Press, 1981).

[30] Christians and Muslims often assume that in Hinduism there is just "polytheism," but this is incorrect. There are many theistic traditions within Hinduism. See, for example, Mariasusai Dhavamony, *Love of God: According to Saiva Siddhanta* (Oxford: Clarendon Press, 1971). As he remarks, "The characteristic note of Tamil Saivism is its strict monotheism, with the conception of God as the Unique Supreme Person. This is in keeping with the bhakti religion, which proposes single-minded and undivided love to the Unique Supreme Being"(337). He continues, "the Saivite theologians do not conceive God's transcendence in such a way as to exclude any relation with the world and men. They repeatedly assert and demonstrate that Siva is not only transcendent but also imminent" (341). See also Bharatan Kumarappa, *The Hindu Conception of the Deity* (Delhi: Inter-India Publications, 1979), where he argues that ". . . the world, consisting of matter and souls is the body of Brahman. He is distinct from it and forms its soul" and "Brahman creates out of free choice, there being no external force constraining Him to create" (210-11).

V
Engaging One Another
A Christian at Eiheiji (Japan)
And Kumsan-Sa (Korea)

Dialogue means more than the exchange of ideas. It also involves the experience of engaging one another, of participating in one another's religious life and practice. Here, I want to share something of my journey into the Buddhist world of life and practice at the temple/monasteries of Eiheiji in Japan and Kumsan-sa in Korea.[1]

Japan: Daimanji and Eiheiji

The fifteen hour flight was long and uneventful. Our approach to Japan was, however, remarkable. The islands were largely covered in cloud, punctuated here and there by black-green mountain tops. The scene that spread beneath me reminded me of the famous sand/rock garden in the Zen temple of Ryoan-ji in Kyoto that I had visited in 1985. It had entranced me then, and it had been the only moment on that journey when my sixteen year old son, Benjamin, became somewhat exasperated with me, remarking, "Dad, how can you just sit here. It's nothing but rocks." This time, my intial intention in coming to Japan had been to visit Kosen Nishiyama, a remarkable Soto Zen priest in Sendai, north of Tokyo. I had met Nishiyama at interfaith conferences and participated in the meditation sessions he had led. I had been drawn to him and wanted to spend some time with him at his Daimanji temple in Sendai. It was only when I arrived in Sendai that I came to know that he had done the first complete translation into English of Dogen's famous *Shobogenzo*.[2] This was doubly interesting to me since, shortly before leaving for Japan, I had received word that it was going to be possible to spend three days at Eiheiji, Dogen's (1200-1253) famous temple/monastery of "Eternal Peace."

I spent several wonderful days with Nishiyama in Sendai, participating in temple life, reading the *Shobogenzo*, and engaging him in conversation about Soto Zen life and practice.[3] Nishiyama had come with me to the airport at Sendai from which I would fly across Japan to the west coast to Komatsu. From there I would take a train to Fukui, then another train up into the mountains to Eiheiji.

Though Dogen had earlier been in Kyoto, he had deliberately abandoned the centre of power for the remote place where Eiheiji is located. As the train wound its way up into the mountains, I read bits and pieces from the Shobogenzo and thought about my time at Sendai with Nishiyama. Each morning at 4:30, we had climbed the two hundred steps up the hill behind his temple to an older temple that was also part of the complex. It was here that we would have our first meditation of the day following the ringing of the bell at 5:00 a.m. Once rung 108 times to symbolize overcoming the desires/ attachments that keep one from Enlightenment, it is now rung a symbolic eighteen times.

The first service in the temple at the top of the hill involved chanting and some remarkable drumming by Nishiyama on a huge drum. The service was dedicated to Kokuzo, a cosmic bodhisattva. During the day there were services in Daimanji, often with only two or three in attendance. Sometimes Nishiyama spoke in English for my sake, but usually the language was Japanese, which I do not understand. Repeatedly, the message that came through from our conversations and his discourses was "Enlightenment comes through practice." Although my practice had involved meditation for some years, it was not in the style or form that I experienced with Nishiyama.

A Buddha-hall at Eiheiji, the Temple of Eternal Peace in Japan

Nishiyama's meditation was the disciplined sitting that Dogen, the founder of the Soto Zen tradition in Japan, had urged. While Nishiyama acknowledged my own Christian convictions, he repeatedly assured me that Dogen's sitting meditation was "non-sectarian" and open to all. He urged me to practice zazen following these three rules: (1) "make proper form," lotus posture with back straight, (2) develop "longer breath," inhaling for ten seconds and exhaling for the same time, and (3) "focus on the mind, try not to think, and come to complete stillness of whole body and whole mind." So every day I did some sitting: at the temple on the top of the hill and in the main Daimanji temple below, sometimes in my room, sometimes on the hilltop.

Although I had visited Zen temples before, this was my first opportunity to be part of an active Soto Zen temple up close. I was surprised to discover the extent to which Daimanji, and the other temples I visited, were "keepers of the dead." Many of the temple activities revolved around services for the ancestors who had died. This connection to the dead was reinforced by the annual O-Bon celebrations that were going on during the time I was in Sendai. The daily life of Daimanji was not as esoteric and as intellectual as many of the texts about Japanese Zen might suggest. I found this comforting.

My dominant recollection of Nishiyama is of his good natured humour. I'll always remember asking him how I should address him. He gave me several options, but then indicated that his foreign students—currently he had two Polish students who had been with him for nearly five years and an American who had been there for two—called him "Hojo San." I laughed and then tried, I'm not sure how successfully, to explain to him the association, to my North American ears, of the title with Howard Johnson's.

The countryside was gradually changing. As we went inland from the sea at Kumatsu, we went through large fields of rice and grains. After we changed trains at Fukui, we began our ascent into the mountains. The August air was humid and heavy, but the passing scene was green and glorious. Japanese pines lined the valley we had climbed as we came to Eiheiji, the small town that had grown up around the temple/monastery, which served mainly those on pilgrimage to Eiheiji.

The walk from the train-station is about a half hour but the heat and the steady climb upward make it seem longer. As I turned up another valley towards the temple-monastery of Eiheiji, I walked along a mountain stream and the sound of cicadas filled the air.

Through the entrance door and I had arrived. The entrance area was filled with tourists/pilgrims (how are they to be distinguished?). I found an "international desk" and was introduced to Reverend Jikisai Minami. He told me that there were three rules in the monastery. The first involved how one held one's hands while walking in the monastery, (left thumb inside palm, right hand over the left as a cover and held at chest height). The second was that silence was to be observed in the bathroom and in the zazen hall. The third concerned the proper way to hold one's hands during zazen: right inside left with the thumbs touching. I told him I wished to fast that day and that I did not want an evening meal. I was then taken to my room. As I passed beyond the entrance hall, the din diminished and the silence and peace of the place began to descend. It was this sense that led me later to write of Eiheiji:

> Buddha beckons
> in moss, and tree, and stone:
> enter within, sit zazen

My room was simple, lovely and spacious. I was left to my own devices for a couple of hours and then a monk came to get me. It turned out he was taking me downstairs to bathe. But how was I to know what he wanted? It was rather humourous since we shared no common words, but through his dramatic gestures and my hunches I finally guessed what we were about. At 6:50 Reverend Minami came by to take me to my first session of zazen. We went down hallways and stairs into a meditation hall where I was given my "pillow," instructed in proper posture, breathing ("four times through the nose and mouth deeply then only through the nose, long and deep"), and ritual. Then I was left for twenty minutes with my nose sixteen inches from the wall. I tried to maintain my posture, focus on my breathing and silently—and probably unBuddhisticly—called on Dogen for assistance and perseverance.

Suddenly, a bell rang and a monk appeared to escort me back to my room. Later that evening, he returned to bring me to Minami's office where I was shown an excellent video on Eiheiji. (Unlike another video done by Japanese television that was scoffing in tone.) It showed Eiheiji through the seasons— roofs with three feet of snow on them in the winter—and something of the young monks in training. Most of the monks there were sons of Soto Zen priests who would eventually return to take over their family's temple. Nishiyama did not come to own Daimanji in this way, but he was hopeful that his son would complete his training at Eiheiji and return to assist him at Daimanji.

Minami and I spent some time discussing the training received at Eiheiji—the young monks usually spend two years here after they have finished a university degree, preferably from one of the Soto Zen universities in Japan. Later, I would continue this conversation with Minami and Rev. Zendo Matsunaga, the head of the International Department. The training at Eiheiji focuses on zazen, ceremonies/rituals, and work. Both felt that there is not enough sutra study at Eiheiji, and they would have liked to see a social dimension added to the training at Eiheiji.

Eiheiji is a large, layered complex that goes up the mountain side. There are probably over twenty buildings in the complex. On my first morning at Eiheiji, Minami gave me the guided tour. We went through the meditation halls, the buddha halls, the entrance halls, the ceremonial halls, the shrine to Dogen, and the kitchens. We walked up long wooden stairs that were roofed but half-open on the sides. Walking around the outside of the halls, along the singing stream that wends its way through Eiheiji, through moss gardens, and under the towering trees, one was reminded again and again that for the Japanese, the sacred is in nature, not beyond it or against it. It is not nature wild but nature swept, as I was reminded when I saw the monks sweeping the moss. It is also nature groomed and shaped to yield its silent witness. Minami told me that I was free to wander about everywhere except for the monks' meditation hall which was off limits. And over the next two days, I did. Later, I was prompted to write of Eiheiji:

who sits?
under your sloping roofs
on boards worn smooth by novice feet
on mats of reed, woven by practiced hands
amidst your towering cedars

beside your verdant moss?

who hears?
the birds among the trees, the talking brook
the quiet breeze, the ringing bell?

silence reigns
it is the temple of eternal peace.
it calls the buddha nature
to blossom.

That first morning I was awake at 2:50, washed and ready when a monk called at 3:30. I was taken to the visitors' meditation hall where that morning there were five others who were part of the meditation—all Japanese men that I placed in their late 50s or early 60s. The silence was deepened by darkness, and incense sweetened the air. Somewhere a bell rang, one gong echoing across the night. We sat: seeking to quiet the internal chatter, to just be, here. Ribbons of pain streaked up unpracticed limbs. Another bell is rung. The session is over.

At 4:50 a.m. I was led up the broad wooden steps to the Ceremonial Hall at the top of Eiheiji. It was a huge room of elegant simplicity. Shades of natural wood rather than the lively colours of the Korean temples created a sense of austerity that was enhanced by the formal entrance of about eighty student/monks who assumed positions along a central aisle leading to the imageless front of the hall. Their turns were precise, their postures rigid, their dress spotless. When the senior members of Eiheiji entered the service commenced. The "Eiheiji Sutras" are chanted and I followed along in my book: "Se son myo so gu ga kon ju mon pi Bus-shi ga in nen myo i kan ze on . . ." through more than forty pages. The sutra-chanting was punctuated by the precise movements of three or four monks lighting incense, bowing in different directions, and performing other ritual gestures. But it was the chanting that dominated. It is impressive. At 5:35 the monks fell out and I returned down the long wooden stairs to my room. Breakfast would be at 6:30.

During the day I followed my own schedule as I wandered around the complex. At times I sat in the Buddha Hall, at others I read the *Shobogenzo*, at others I sat in the moss garden near Dogen's shrine, Joyoden. It was there that I wrote:

This is Dogen's place
here time stands still, caught by tranquility
born of zazen

waters flow
the air heavy with summer
the moss a coverlet on the earth
the rocks remember "being-time"
there is no other place.
just sit.

we are here.
satori.

And later I wrote of Dogen,

Echoing across the centuries:
"drop mind-body!"
follow the way:

sit.
It knows not time, nor space, nor place.

IT IS:
ringing eternity, shimmering clouds
murmuring waters, glowing moss.

speaking beyond words
silence, zazen

That evening I again joined Minami for a conversation. This time the conversation began with a discussion of the limitations of language in relation to religious experience and ontology. Minami reminded me that the Zen tradition is very leery of language, fearful that we will confuse the pointing finger with the moon to which it is pointing. The conversation then turned to "deconstruction"—which he finds rather confusing—and the connections that have been drawn between it and Buddhism in general and Dogen in particular. We shared a laugh about the common ground we discovered in our confusion concerning deconstructionist writings. Minami admitted that some strands of Buddhism share the deconstructionist critique of language and concepts. But he made the essential point that Dogen's famous "Uji-essay" on "Being-time" is grounded in the practice of zazen, of meditation, and not in some speculative nihilism as seems to be the case in deconstruction.

I returned to my room for some sitting meditation before I unrolled my bedding on the tatami mat. The rich memories of the day passed through my mind as I quickly went to sleep.

When I left Eiheiji to return to Tokyo, the experience of the monks of Eiheiji stayed with me. I later wrote:

They sit in silence, backs straight,
eyes open but not looking,
softly breathing, moving within,
heeding rhythms unseen,
practicing enlightenment.

Outside trees grow,
moss spreads, birds ride the wind,
water dances down the rocks, air moves unseen
as silence speaks:
beyond words, in rhythms deep within.

No outside, nor inside,
both beyond,
yet within.
They sit in silence.

It had been a moving experience and one that extended and deepened my sense of the Buddhist Way.

Korea: Kumsan-sa Shimwon-am

Chonju is located about three hours south of Seoul by express bus. South of Chonju, a smaller highway winds its way up the valleys, through small villages, in the direction of Mt. Kum. In late August, the roadside is covered with red peppers drying in the hot sun. The rice fields are a deep green. There are signs of harvest in the terraced gardens and tiny fields that line the valleys. As the local bus twisted and turned through the villages of the valleys, always going up, I was entranced by the beauty of rural Korea. Finally we came to the large parking area outside the temple/monastery of Kumsan-sa, one of Korea's most well-known. Kumsan-sa or Mount Kum Temple was founded in 599 AD and has been the site of Buddhist practice ever since. It is part of the Chogye Order of Korean Buddhism, an order which embraces all the traditional sects.[5] It is famous for its three-story temple, the only one in Korea, that houses a thirty foot Maitreya Buddha.

The way up to Kumsan-sa from the parking lot passes through a gate which puts us on a path that winds through cherry trees and along a stream. In August, the blossoms are long gone, and the air hot and humid, but as I walked the kilometer to the temple, I was aware that I had left one world behind and entered another. A sense of tranquility began to descend as I walked along the still bubbling stream with its song of water dancing over the stones and heard the cicadas—"mamies" in Korean I was told—sang their August songs. Half way to the temple is another gate, a single-poled gate in the primary greens, blues, and reds that are so typical of Korean Buddhist sites. This gate, my guide Han Tap Sunim, a Buddhist monk, informed me, symbolizes the non-dualist beliefs of Buddhism, the conviction that reality is one. Nearer the temple we passed pilgrims leaving the site and a family down by the stream cooling their feet in the rushing waters. As we walked under the gatehouse that stands at the entrance to the complex of Kumsan-sa, we heard the sounds of wood blocks and chant. It was a taped recording, linking this ancient site with the world of modern technology. Around the large dusty square, under the hot August sun of late afternoon, were six temples, including the three-story Maitreya Temple currently being restored and a beautiful new Buddha Hall that faces one across the square. Behind the complex, the green mountains continued to rise, giving the whole setting a feel of being nestled in the bosom of a glorious nature.

For the next days, I would be living here in a space saturated by centuries of practice and the daily round of the twenty monks currently in residence. Han Tap Sunim has proven to be a wonderful surprise. I had not anticipated finding someone who spoke English, nor was I prepared for the moving account of Buddhist belief I received from him over the following days. One of the most memorable conversations included Han Tap's explanation of Buddhism. According to Han Tap,

... our fate is formed through karma. And, according to the Zen sect, we can attain perfect liberation and overcome karma through meditation.

"But," he wondered, "what about the lay person? We have found," he continued, "that Buddha has transfered his merit to all sentient beings and when we call 'na mu a mi ta bul' we are calling on Buddha's merit. Buddha's enlightenment was not for himself, but for all creation! And since our lives are taken up in the Buddha's life, we can attain Buddhahood by calling on his name." For, he concluded with that infectious smile, "Buddha is life." (Later I read in Dogen's Shobogenzo these words: "Life and death itself is the life of Buddha" (678).

This wonderful expression of a Pure Land faith led me later to write,

NAMU
As the Morning Star rises and the Buddha awakens,
the Cosmos sings and all Sentient Beings rejoice.
NA-MU-A-MI-TA-BUL
NA-MU-A-MI-TA-BUL
NA-MU-A-MI-TA-BUL
. . . on and on.
It is a mercy chant, echoing across the sky
tieing night to day, Living to Dead, All to All
in the dawn of Pure Land.

I later wrote a poem for Han Tap:

a human stupa, a pagoda raised up
living faith not dead bones.

at sixty he took the Buddha way:
a simple life, a holy way, an enlightened play.

now "dharma master"
preaching a Buddha enlightened for all
and living boundless life.

joy breaks across his face, lighting a million lights:
suffering overcome, mercy made real
Buddha come home.

he's a believer true.
living Buddha's mercy
in all, for all.

Nor was I prepared for the further surprises that awaited
me. For now I turned my attention to a round of meditation,
rest, silence, and reflection as I participated in the life of this
lovely temple/monastery. Each day I rose at 2:45 a.m. to go to
the Buddha Hall for the service and chanting. Then I remained
for my solitary meditation including a meditative walk under
the stars as the dawn came. During the day I read in my
room, continued my conversations with Han Tap, and

Abbess Cho-ui Sunim and Chomal-sun at a
retreat at Shimwon-am, South Korea

meditated in the halls around the central courtyard, retiring
by 9:00 p.m. Of the magical beginning of each day, I wrote:

3:00 AM

Across the darkened night the wood block sounds
the bell rings, the gong soars, the drum beats
shattering the stillness of sleeping night
bearing prayer to all sentient beings.

now
eternal rhythm
sounds:
a bolt across the sky, a flash within the mind
warmth around the heart.

we rise, drawn by an enlightened beat
that beats as one with Buddha heart

And then after a walk along the mountain stream, I wrote:

One Moon
one Buddha
alive in a thousand streams
tumbling down the mountain side,

silent in still waters
mirroring a silver light.

All sing one song:
AWAKE.

Shimwon/Cho-ui Sunim

On my third day at Kumsan-sa, Han Tap suggested a walk further up the valley toward the mountain. As we went out the back-gate of Kumsan-sa, we passed crocks full of soya sauce and kimchi (the spiced cabbage that is a staple at every Korean meal) and took a road that wound through gardens and orchards lined with rose-of-sharon bushes. The way up the mountain led us along a stream that danced with cool water and sang its songs as it skipped along its boulder filled course. The road, a layer of concrete wide enough for a Korean jeep, went up the mountain towards a broadcasting station perched near its peak. But about twenty minutes away from Kumsan-sa, a path led off to the left leading to Shimwon-am. Han Tap mentioned that it was a very small temple.

The way up to Shimwon-am was very steep, and in the late morning heat, I wondered if it would be worth the effort. Although the sign said it was only a half-kilometer away, it seemed much further as we walked up the twisting path that doubled back on itself under a cover of trees and pines. On the way we passed an ancient burial site, the round-topped domes of the past, that was obviously still cared for. After a couple of more turns, we finally came to a little jewel of a temple called Shimwon-am. It is simple of line, modest in size. It sits up on a terraced courtyard, entered up eight stone steps in the front. To the immediate right of the temple is a

113

beautiful series of stone pools that catch the water from a spring for drinking and bathing. Further off the raised terrace, on both the left and right, are well-tended gardens. Around Shimwon lies the stillness of the mountain, its shades of green and a welcome breeze. The place is pervaded by a sense of serenity and peace, even though two puppies, one brown and one white, nosily announced our arrival.

We were greeted by the Abbess, Cho-ui Sunim. I was immediately struck by her inner calm, her gentle presence as she welcomed us to her temple. After entering the temple to pay respects to the Buddha image there, we were invited to take a seat on the veranda that stretches across the front of the temple for a drink and lunch. Although we did not share a common language, Cho-ui Sunim communicated a great deal through her presence and her actions. She and Han Tap conversed in Korean as I got my bearings in the beautiful place we had come to. The deep inward peace one sensed in the Abbess was mirrored in the tranquility of the setting. It was clear that she has laboured hard to make the little temple— an "am" rather than a "sa" to indicate its small size—and the grounds a place that is serene. Her efforts were written in her hands which tell you that her labour is physical as well as mental and inward. Later I learned that she had been there for two years and is the first resident priest in some time.

Cho-ui Sunim had someone with her, an older woman, Chomal-sun, on a hundred day devotion/retreat. Together, they quickly extended their lunch to include these two unexpected visitors. Seated on the veranda, we enjoyed a delightful lunch of rice and vegetables while I learned something of Cho-ui. She studied and trained at Hein-sa, one of the largest and most important Chogye/Zen-centres in Korea and the site of the carved wood blocks of the whole Buddhist canon. There she had spent thirteen years, and this was the first temple where she had been in charge.

Her day begins at 2:15 a.m. when she rises for a 3:00 a.m. service followed by a period of meditation. In the daylight hours of summer, she tends her gardens to raise her own food, gathers wood for the winter, and looks after the temple site. In the spring and autumn, some hikers and climbers stop in, but mostly she is alone. When I asked her if she gets lonely, she just smiled quietly and said "a Zen nun cannot feel that way." Cho-ui had decided to become a Buddhist nun when she read about the teachings of the Buddha while she was attending high school. Since then, she has dedicated her life to the Buddhist way. The only sounds in her life these days are the "mamies and birds." She struck me as a delightful human being, self-contained yet responsive, at peace. She went on to say that she very much enjoys the "red world" of autumn and the "white world" of winter. I imagine her there in the snow covered mountains of winter, deep in meditation, with a hint of a smile across her face.

The name of her temple, Shimwon, means "Deep Origins," so hers is the "Little Temple [am] of Deep Origins." It is a wonderful name. While there, we sat in meditation in the simple meditation room with its golden Buddha image and the brightly coloured and beautiful painting. I learned that the altar painting was done by the son of the woman, Chomal-sun, doing a retreat. His name is Kang Hae Jwo, he is 28 and obviously very gifted. His strong colours, traditional images, and sense of proportion make this a painting worthy of meditative attention. After a couple of hours, we take our leave to return to Kumsan-sa, but with a promise that I will return in the early morning for meditation.

I'm overwhelmed by it all—the temple, the setting, the people who encapsulate the depth and beauty of Buddhism in such an impressive way. It exceeds words.

The following morning, I returned alone to Shimwon-am. Han Tap has had to leave for other duties. Again the way is steep, but the early morning coolness makes it an easier climb. Again, the dogs announce my coming. When I was here yesterday, I learned that some months earlier, a Korean Christian had broken into the temple and damaged the

115

Buddha image. I had been appalled by the story, and thus I returned this morning partly to redress this bad faith of a fellow-Christian and to pay my respects to her Buddhist way which has taught me so much. We bow to each other, to the Buddha image in the temple and exchange a Korean greeting but that exhausts my knowledge of the language. (Yesterday, Cho-ui had laughingly chided herself for failing to pay sufficient attention to her high school classes in English.) With gestures and words I do not comprehend, Cho-ui Sunim invites me to take a seat for tea. She then proceeds to prepare the tea of the front veranda while the puppies become easy in my presence. My page of "Survival Korean" quickly proves hopeless—its composed of phrases, requests, that are appropriate to getting by in a city like Seoul, but hardly suitable for an exchange about the Buddhist Way here in Shimwon. Although I do learn the names for her puppies—Hanul (heaven) and Kurum (cloud)—and the word for "beautiful," since it most comes to my lips to describe what I am seeing, our tea unfolds in silence. It is broken only by the swish of water in the tea pot as each small cup of tea is individually prepared. After tea, the three of us go into the temple to meditate. There in the silence of this sacred space one realizes the ignorance that would separate the space within from the space of the temple and that of the mountainside without. Here they all flow into one another in an emptiness that exceeds us all. The silence speaks in its own way and must be heard within, if at all.

It is a place of "deep origins." It is a place to meet a remarkable Buddhist woman. It is a place where temple and nature, silence and meditation, work in the gardens within and without, meet and embrace each other.

As I leave, I realize I have been in a very special place and with a person of special presence. I have been moved by my experience and its imprint will remain long after details begin to fade. I later wrote this poem of my visit to Shimwon:

116

Beside the laughing stream runs a path,
going the other way.
It leads up, the mountain way
past fields of rice, flowering trees, pines stretched high.

the way grows/harder, the path
twists back
on itself
until it becomes
an echo, an emblem of another journey,
that twists and turns in human hearts.

Set high on mountain brow,
ringed round by nature's glory
her lines a compliment to nature's way:
Shimwom, the deep, high place.

Endnotes

[1] Eric Newby and Laurens vander Post are two of my favourite writers. Newby is an English travel writer of many books including *A Short Walk in the Hindu Kush*, *Slowly Down the Ganges*, and *A Small Place in Italy*. His writings are marked by good humour and a sensitivity to the life and places he is writing about. Laurens vander Post was a South African whose many novels and books include *Venture to the Interior*, *The Lost World of the Kalahari*, and *The Heart of the Hunter*. His writings also often involve journeys and travel. His *Venture to the Interior* is at once an account of an exploration of Nyasaland (now Malawi) and of the human psyche. His *Lost World of the Kalahari* and *The Heart of the Hunter* present the search for the people of the Kalahari, the Bushman peoples (or, as the anthropologists prefer, the !Kung) and their religious way.

Their writings, it occured to me, point to what I am about here: a journey, as a student of religion and a Christian, into the Buddhist world. It strikes me that that is often what we are about as students of religion: seeking to describe religious worlds with sympathy and hopefully some insight. And this is so, at least for me, in the dialogue of Buddhism and Christianity, which as

Wilfred Cantwell Smith continually reminds us, is a dialogue of persons who are Buddhists and Christians. As I see it, part of that dialogue in engaging one another's religious life and practice. It is such engagement that leads to a deepened understanding of each other's religious way.

² Dogen Zenji, *Shobogenzo: The Eye and Treasury of the True Law,* trans. Kosen Nishiyama (Tokyo: Nakayama Shobo/Japan Publications Trading Co., 1975).This remarkable collection of discourses and essays ranges widely from "Great Enlightenment" to "The Rule for Zazen" and "Rules for the Lavatory."

³ See D. T. Suzuki, *Zen and Japanese Buddhism* (Tokyo: Japan Travel Bureau, 1970), esp. pp. 41ff.

⁴ See Ninian Smart, *The World's Religions* (NJ: Prentice-Hall and Chai-Shin Yu, ed., *Korean and Asian Religious Tradition* (Toronto: University of Toronto Press, 1977).

VI
The Kumbha Mela
A Festival and Sacred Place

The Kumbha Mela), a festival held in North India, at the conjunction of the Jamuna and Ganges rivers at Allahabad (Prayag) every twelve years is the world's largest religious and human gathering. Unfortunately, there is little written in English about the Kumbha Mela.[1] And as a student of religion since the early 60s, I must admit that I was not aware of the Kumbha Mela before 1987 when I learned about it from Shrivatsa Goswami of Vrindaban. It was this chance encounter—and Shrivatsa's generous invitation to be part of his family's camp at the Kumbha Mela—that led me to attend the Kumbha Mela in 1989[2] and again in 2001. Some have described this event as "the world's largest act of faith."[3] In this essay I would like to both describe some of what I encountered at the Kumbha Mela and highlight some questions that the event poses for the student of religion. I also discuss how I view my participation in the Kumbha Mela as part of the dialogue of persons of different faiths. Let me begin with some of the questions and issues that face the student of religion when encountering the Kumbha Mela.

What Is It? Festival, Pilgrimage, Sacred Place?

A first and basic question—and the one students always ask me when I show them the video that I made of the Kumbha Mela—is: what is the Kumbha Mela? I know that I can always

Pilgrims at the Ganges River during the Kumbha Mela, 2001

say, it is "the Festival of the Pitcher" but is this adequate? Isn't it also a place of pilgrimage?[4] This was what was said to me by Raj Kumar and two other villagers from Bihar who had walked to the Kumbha Mela in 1989: "We have come on a pilgrimage and to bathe in the Ganga." But it is a place of pilgrimage with a difference. How is it different from places of pilgrimage like Santiago de Compostela in Spain? Or the *haj* to Mecca? Or climbing Mt. Fuji in Japan? These are all spatially fixed places of pilgrimage—though two are historically created sites and one is a natural site. The place that is the site of the Great or Maha Kumbha Mela is a special place of pilgrimage only at certain times—about once every twelve years. At other times it remains a holy place, as the rivers Ganga and Yamuna are always sacred rivers. But at those times it is not what it becomes during a Maha Kumbha Mela. And while people may come here on pilgrimage during the times when this juncture of the two rivers is swollen or flooded with the waters of the monsoon or when it is a dry and dusty flood plain, it is not what it becomes during the Kumbha Mela.

The Kumbha Mela as a place of pilgrimage is as much an event as it is a place and a time. It is an event sanctioned by a particular solar constellation—which determines the dates on which the Festival takes place—and linked to the presence of the holy men and women—sadhus, gurus, mahaswamis, acharyas, etc.—that come to camp here at this time. But it also requires the millions of pilgrims who come to bathe in these holy waters at this auspicious time, to sit at the feet of their gurus, to perform countless acts of *puja*, to watch holy dramas enacted, to read and study holy books, to meditate, and do the myriad other things that take place during this time.[5] It is a conjunction of time, place, and people that make the Kumbha Mela, but in ways that are unique and unrepeatable even though this event has been occuring, some say, for the last couple of millennia.[6] It is a complex and multivalent event more than a place.

Jack Hebner and David Osborn in their book on the Kumbha Mela call it—and I have used the phrase above— "the world's largest act of faith." It is surely true that it is the largest—indeed, it dwarfs all other analogous religious events like the *haj* to Mecca or the Easter gatherings in front of St. Peter's Basilica in Rome—but the authors' account of the "faith" present at the Kumbha Mela is disappointing. And while such a description points to the remarkable numbers that are present for the Kumbha Mela, it does not clarify its purposes and intentions. To get at those dimensions of the Kumbha Mela it is necessary to probe into the stories in the sacred texts of Hinduism and into the minds of the pilgrims who come to the Kumbha Mela.

When we turn to those sacred texts we discover a wide variety of accounts of mythological stories and events that help us towards understanding the inner purposes of the Kumbha Mela. For example, in the *Rig Veda* we are told that those that "bathe at the confluence of the white waters of the

Ganga and the black waters of the Yamuma go to the celestial heavens." (Khila-svalayana) And the Garuda Purana (Arca-Kanda 81.2) says that Prayaga is "a very holy place conducive to worldly enjoyment and liberation . . . by taking a bath there, all sins are dispelled."[7] In several of the ancient texts we discover the story of the churning of the ocean of milk and the resulting appearance of a "pitcher" containing a "nectar of immortality." In the Bhagavad Purana, one of the sacred texts of the Hindu traditions, the story is told of how the appearance of this pitcher of nectar provoked such a clamour on the earth that a messenger of the gods grabbed the pitcher and returned it to the heavens. (Another story says the demigods hid it at certain spots.) But in her flight back to the Beyond, some drops of the nectar of immortality fell to the earth. (One account says 11 spots, four in India.) One of those spots where the nectar touched the earth was at the confluence of these two sacred rivers: the Yamuna and Ganges. But the mythic story also adds a third, even more powerful river to the two geographical rivers, the invisible Saraswati. Thus the site of this great festival is at the confluence of three rivers, rivers that are at once human and divine.

This mythic background points to one of the significant features of the festival as a sacred place. For the believer, this environment has been touched by divine gifts: it is here in this place that the nectar of immortality was spilled and not somewhere else. Thus it is to this spot that Hindus from across India come to participate in the festival. It is, as we indicated earlier, a place where the human and divine have been joined, and thus it is a place where human transformation can occur. But to the eye unformed by the mythic story, the site could be mistaken for a large sandy plain along two rivers.[8]

Thus far we can see that we can speak of the Kumbha Mela as a place/event of pilgrimage and as the world's largest gathering, but isn't it also important to see it as a sacred place? When we approach it in this way, we highlight the role that sacred spaces have played in the story of humankind.

From time immemorial, men and women have made pilgrimages to sacred places. Those sacred places may be, as we noted above, natural as in the case of Mt. Fuji in Japan, or Lha-moi La-tso Lake in Tibet or Mount Kenya in Africa.[9] Or they may be constructed sites like the Shrine at Fatima, the Cathedral at Chartres, the City of the Sun (Machu Pichu) in Peru or the Sweat Lodge of the Plains Indian. But this sacred place is both a natural place and a constructed place. Humankind across the planet has gathered to celebrate in festivals the meeting of divine and human life, or what Mircea Eliade has called "the manifestation of the sacred."[10] Religious festivals have been a feature of the human landscape in times past and present, East and West.

Observing/Participating in the Kumbha Mela

Here I want to report some of my observations on the Kumbha Melas that I attended in 1989 and in 2001. Elsewhere you can find a fuller account of the circumstances that brought me to the Kumbha Mela in 1989, but let me begin with my arrival at the Kumbha Mela in 1989.

I arrived in Allahabad as the sun was setting. I was met by Venu Goswami, a younger brother of Shrivatsa . . . . As we drove to the Kumbha Mela, Venu spoke about what lay ahead. In the hour-long journey, we found ourselves increasingly in the midst of a flood of humanity moving, in a variety of ways, towards the same destination . . . . As we neared the camp, the road was choked with pilgrims on their way to the Kumbha Mela, their worldly goods balanced atop their heads as they resolutely made their way to the banks of the sacred rivers. We finally came out through the city walls only to be confronted by a vast network of street lights that stretched as far as we could see over the camped city. Venu informed me that the grounds covered a 20 square kilometer area, and at this hour it was shrouded in the smoke of camp fires but alive with the booming

123

microphones and loudspeaker systems that would be a
constant feature of my days at the Kumbha Mela.[11]

Thus from the very outset, one was confronted by the
reality of pilgrims making their way to a sacred place and I
wondered if I was one of them. Amidst the remarkable
diversity of sites and structures that have been regarded as
sacred places by different religious communities and cultures,
there is an equally remarkable consistency of purpose. Sacred
places in widely different parts of the world share either one
or all of the characteristic functions of sacred places. They are
either places of communion between the human and divine,
or places of power where human life might be transformed,
or places that reflect or embody the sacred order of the divine,
or all three of these.[12] And even as I wondered about my own
status in this place, I was made aware over the coming days
that the Kumbha Mela was all of these things.

The scale of the Kumbha Mela is daunting: the camp-city
along the rivers, the numbers of pilgrims, and the variety of
activities occurring at the Festival. Joel Beverton has observed
the close connection that exists between sacred places and
rituals. This is especially true at the Kumbha Mela where
daily life is filled with ritual activity, beginning with the ritual
bathing in the Ganga, the rituals conducted at the rivers as
lamps and offering are placed in the sacred waters, in the
camps before the enshrined dieties, and in other, countless
ways. Beverton has observed that the rituals "that a people
either practice at a place or direct toward it mark its sacredness
and differentiate it from other defined spaces."[13] But it is critical
to remember that rituals, like sacred places, are not always
places that can be entered physically. They are not always
sacred lands or temples or churches or mountains. Sacred places
may also be places that one must enter imaginatively, as in
the inner geography of the body in yoga, or visually, as in the
space of a mandala or sacred design. Similarly, rituals are not

only outward gestures and actions, but they are also an inner environment of the mind and imagination.

But it is difficult to understand the outward gestures and actions if you do not know or share the inner environment of the pilgrim. While it is possible to describe the outer environment of this sacred place, the inner environment that the pilgrim brings with him or her is more difficult to comprehend. The simple response of Ram Sharma—"I am a pilgrim, I've come to bathe in the Ganga"—was the same one that I received from others time and again. Acts and gestures of piety and devotion reflecting a special inner environment were what I observed and recorded on my first morning at the river's edge, and throughout the Festival in both 1989 and 2001:

At the river, people are doing their morning ablutions. Occasionally, a flute being played somewhere cuts through the noise with its plaintive welcome to the new day. I also hear the blowing of a conch. The fiery red ball of the sun begins to peek over the horizon, shedding its multi-coloured hues through the haze and smoke that hangs over the camp. By the water, pilgrims go in and out, many with their lips moving in the rhythms of a silent mantra as the new day began. Some place sticks of incense in the sand and it wafts across the stirring camp. As I sit by the water watching the rising sun and the increasing bustle around me, I find myself meditating on the wonder and beauty of it all.

On another occasion I wrote,

Here, a constant stream of men, women, and children enter the river, chanting and praying. Garlands of flowers are offered to the river along with tiny clay vessels of oil that are lit and placed in the river. As I criss-cross the camp, I am being drawn into this extraordinary event, watching the ceaseless flow of human beings; stopping to observe a sadhu seated before a fire with his trident, sign of Shiva, placed beside him; bemused by children gathered around a spigot washing some clothes and throwing water at one another; noting the colourful saris being dried while held by two human clotheslines; witnessing countless acts of puja (worship). It is unlike anything I have ever witnessed before.

Over the days I was at the Festival, I sought to enter into the inner environment that was present there as well as the outer place. This requires imagination if one is to go into the inner sacred places where the pilgrims live. It also sometimes required a translator, but I was able to speak to many in English.

What I began to grasp is what scholars of religion call the "places of power" function of sacred spaces: that is, the conviction among the pilgrims that in these places "human life might be transformed." Clearly, that was part of the conviction as pilgrims entered the flowing waters of Mother Ganga. Here are some of my observations from 6 February 1989 as the Kumbha Mela came to be focused on the Sangam on this most auspicious day.

Off in the east, the bright ball of the sun inched up the horizon and a roar went up from the crowd: the human world rose up to greet the sun that spreads its crimson rays on this new day. As the sun rose, one could feel the mounting energies. A rush of joy seemed to ripple through the surging crowds. And the sunrise was beautiful: that ball of flaming red rose through the dust and haze like a jewel to refract its light on all. It revealed a humanity that spread as far as I could see along the banks of the rivers and beyond. And, for a moment, the moving waters and the ebb and flow of the humanity gathered there seemed to dance with one another in perfect harmony as the sun rose over it all. The pilgrims, nameless and numberless, were making their way to the waters, entering those waters, then returning to the banks and there changing their clothes, visiting with others, then making their way to those countless places they had come from. Had they been renewed? Cleansed? freed from sin? Purified? Strengthened on their road to moksha or liberation? I could not judge; I could only wonder as I stood there transfixed by this sea of humanity in motion in response to promptings that could not be seen but could be felt . . . .

In 2001, there was a greater attempt to manage access to the Sangam, the meeting point of the rivers, than there had been in 1989—and the police presence at the Sangam was much more evident. Though the numbers for 2001 were said to be some 4 to 6 million more than in 1989, this was not evident at the Sangam in 2001. The site was ripped by a cold wind that had blown throughout the night. And my own walk to the Sangam, together with a dozen others from the Gambira Ashram where I stayed was more difficult due to the police management of the site. Indeed, at one point I was pulled to the side for carrying a camera. "No pictures, no press," the policeman told me. When I assured him I was not press, he let me continue.

This sacred place, the setting of the festival, is not marked by soaring mountains or other dramatic geographic features. Alongside the rivers are sandy flood plains where the rivers annually overrun their banks. The two rivers that meet here have their origins hundreds of kilometers away in the Himalayas. From their beginnings high in the mountains, they make their way across the northern plains of India to Allahabad, known to many by its ancient Hindu name of Prayag, where they join. From their headwaters in the Himalayas and all along the way, these rivers are marked by places of pilgrimage where believers come to worship and to bathe in their sacred waters.

In India, with its rich Hindu heritage and culture, rivers have often been regarded in more than human terms. Rivers bespeak another language, one that is articulated in the myths

Author, Sri Purushottam, Smt Sandhya, Sri Shrivatsa Goswami at the Kumbha Mela, 2001

and legends of Indian life. In past millenia, people gathered at Stonehenge for festivals we still do not fully understand — and recently "New Age" groups have begun to gather there again. In Canada, Native peoples, Algonquin and Mohawk, regarded the 1000 Islands as a "garden of the gods," and journeyed there to dance on the rocky islands. The celebration of Easter draws hundreds of thousands to Jerusalem to walk the places that Jesus had walked. But when we seek to understand these events, it is necessary to grasp the inner environment that the pilgrims bring to these events.

Accessing the Inner Environment: Purushottam

One of the problems for me in attempting to understand the Kumbha Mela is that the Indian participants share an inner environment of belief and gesture that was not mine. How could I come to "see" what was happpening here? Religious festivals have social, archetypal, and cosmic dimensions that are all combined in remarkably compressed gestures and actions or elaborately dramatized in extended performative acts. The difficulty of grasping the inner meanings of this event is related to the most remarkable feature this sacred place: the ever-flowing waters of the Ganga and Yamuna. And to get to those meanings I was dependent upon the insight of the participants who shared those patterns of belief that gave meaning to what I was witnessing. Earlier, Sri Jagadguru Purushottam Goswami, Shrivatsa's father and head of the community, shared with us a discourse on the Kumbha Mela in which he explained that the Festival is a ritual of purification and renewal. Through the centuries, believers had gathered on the banks of these sacred rivers, he explained, to be renewed by offering their *puja* to Mother Ganga and listening to the discourses of their teachers and bathing in the Ganga. For him, the Festival is a retreat, a time for self-examination and meditation, for reading the sacred writings, for performing acts of devotion and worship to Lord Krishna. In 2001 I was again able to meet with Sri Purushottam and he provided a remarkable discourse on the Khumba Mela, some of which is reported here. His words were translated from Hindi into English by his son, Shrivatsa Goswami:

> This place is unique because the nectar of immortality has rained on this place. And devotees gather here to gather that nectar. And what is that nectar? It is devotion to the Lord. Bhakti, or love and devotion to God, is the only proper way, the only proper devotion. And it is only through that devotion—a devotion wholly without selfishness—that we gain God, that we gain immortality. The only purpose, then, of the Kumbha Mela is to focus on loving service to God.

I then asked him to explain how that "loving service" that is the purpose of the Kumbha Mela is related to bathing in the river Ganga? Sri Purushottam responded,

> When the Ganga, the nectar of immortality, was about to descend from the heavens it wondered: if I come to earth who will revere me? And won't everyone pollute me? But Ganga was reassured: Shiva, the greatest of all

devotees will receive you on his head. And it was Shiva's devotion that persuaded the Ganga to come to earth. And yet the Ganga waited for years to come, she waited for devotees to offer their devotion to the Ganga. The Ganga will cleanse the devotees and their devotion will cleanse the Ganga. Ganga thus came as an act of grace and their loving service will overcome the pollution that the Ganga will receive.

He then continued with a longer discussion of the rivers that meet at the Sangam: the Ganga, the Yamuna, and the Saraswati. He said that the Kumbha Mela was a moment of relishing for all the rivers, as they received the devotion of their devotees. When the Kumbha Mela happens "the rivers are happy when they can hear, in singing and in stories, the devotion of devotees."

Sri Purushottam, himself a devotee of Krishna and Radha, explained that,

> The model for the Kumbha Mela is Lord Ram. He shows us how we should approach the rivers, how we should approach and bathe in the river. After Lord Ram had been banished, he was driven on a chariot though the forest when he saw the glow of the Ganga from afar. First he got down . . . then he fell prostrate on the ground. Thereafter he gave up the ride and walked barefoot. When the Ganga is visible then you should not walk with shoes on to the river. But you should go barefoot, in humility, in devotion . . . This is the code of conduct that should be observed. Exhibition bathing is not the Kumbha Mela, loving devotion is. . . .

The Ganga is our mother and she is compassionate, not just to her children but to all. Her loving power is witnessed by many. At Benares one morning, some ladies entered the waters and some people saw a herd of deer and a chariot flying to heaven. It was not a surprise. Ganga explained that whoever comes in contact with me will be redeemed, will get relief from their bondage. (The ladies had used musk for their unguent and the deer providing the musk were travelling to heaven!) This is the unrestricted compassion of the mother ...

It is possible to sense the devotion as one watches the pilgrims make their way to the water's edge and enter a river that is, for them, more than a river. It is a living symbol of divine grace that flows and renews constantly those who enter its transforming waters.

But Sri Purushottam also made the point that for the mutual cleansing of the rivers and the devotees to occur, it was essential for the heart of the devotee to be rightly focused. In his words,

The Kumbha Mela is the festival of pots (kumbha means a pot). Though the Ganga is so compassionate, it is also important that your heart, the pot, be empty of arrogance and pride. Those who bathe seeking prestige through the holy gift will not receive the holy gift. How could they? Their hearts are already filled with the poison of ambition and so Ganga will not be able to enter ... Those who come in purity and humility will be renewed for it is humility that makes us open. But arrogance, ambition, and pride are the opposite of loving service and close the heart.[14]

Throughout my time at the Kumbha Mela, I found myself continually trying to discern the meaning of what I was witnessing. The questions I had exceeded my answers, and I found myself drawn again and again to the rivers since it was obviously the rivers that constituted the heart of this sacred place:

I returned again to the river, upstream from the Sangam, and watched again the pilgrims there performing their puja on the banks of "Mother Ganga." The river flowed by, flowers were cast on its endless currents, incense was stuck in the bank, pilgrims entered and dipped themselves the ceremonial three times, the ritual continued. It went on as it has for centuries. I found myself wondering if I was watching an eternal drama, one that would continue as long as humanity remains aware of its need for renewal, for purification, for the revival of the spirit. I wondered as I watched again as the streaming waters of the Ganga met the streaming masses of humanity in the wonderful dance where outer meets inner and becomes a living symbol of something more.

Here are my reflections on my last day at the Kumbha Mela, two days after the "day of days."

I made my way to the river for my final farewells. I felt I wanted to be at the river one last time, to see once again the cycle of pilgrims coming to and from the river, performing their acts of worship, continuing the rhythms that mark this extraordinary event. I can see that Mother Ganga is more than just another river. It is the living presence of the mystery of life's origins and continuities as it ceaselessly flows towards its destiny. It is moving to watch the reverence with which it is approached, entered, and acknowledged through time-honoured rituals. The river is, as it were, an endlessly flowing symbol of grace that renews as it cleanses, that transforms as it receives. For the pilgrim, it seems to have a power, presence, and a persona that is difficult for me to grasp, though I can glimpse it in their acts of devotion. And I find it very moving. There is even a moment when I feel caught up in the archetypal drama as the endless round of pilgrims meet and enter its endless flowing waters. But then it draws away.

The Multivalent Event

At the outset, we pointed to the scholarly readings of the functions of sacred places and places of pilgrimage. We noted that they function as (1) places of communication, (2) places of power, and (3) places that embody. It is possible to see all these functions occuring at the Kumbha Mela. At the heart of this sacred place and Festival are the waters of the Ganga and Yamuna. Water has always had a primordial significance within the religious life of humankind. It is a multivalent symbol. It is, in the words of the Bhavisyottara Purana, "the source of all things and all existence."[15] It is, at the same time, the renewer and purifier of all. It is a living water. When this rich symbolism of water is combined with the symbolism of immersion in the water, then we are moving closer to a central feature of this Festival. Eliade remarks that:

> . . . in water everything is "dissolved", every "form" is broken up, everything that has happened ceases to exist; nothing that was before remains after immersion in water . . . . Immersion is the equivalent, at the human level, of death, and at the cosmic level, of the cataclysm which periodically dissolves the world . . . . Breaking all forms, doing away with all the past, water possesses this power of purifying, of regenerating, of giving new birth; for what is immersed in it "dies", and, rising again from the water, is like a child without any sin or any past, able to . . . begin a new and real life." [16]

When seen in this light, the sacred "Mother Ganga" begins to disclose her place in the life of India and the traditions that have shaped her inner environment. In this Festival, the waters of the rivers are at once the living waters of purification, of grace, renewal, and transformation. And immersion in the "Mother," which is at once the visible Ganga and Yamuna and the invisible Saraswati, is the ritual action that transforms. The pilgrimage to this sacred place coupled with the transforming power and presence of the sacred waters combine to make the Festival of the Pitcher a remarkable festival, a remarkable sacred place, and a remarkable place of pilgrimage.

It is a place where the rivers flow on and on, reflecting the light of the sun's rising and setting, and carrying with them the offerings of devoted hearts—flowers and oil-lit lamps—as they silently continue their endless journey.

Endnotes

[1] See, for example, the entry one finds in Ninian Smart's *The World's Religions* (Englewood Cliffs, NJ: Prentice-Hall, 1989), "We see India drawn together by great pilgrimages, at Banaras and at the vast Kumbh Mela fair at Prayag, where the rivers Jumna and Ganges meet the invisible river Sarasvati" (100). There is surprisingly little written in the literature of religious studies on the Kumbha Mela. An exception is the moving contemporary interpretation of the Festival found in Sehdev Kumar's *The Lotus in the Stone: An Allegory for Explorations in Dreams and Consciousness* (Concord, Ontario: Alpha & Omega Books, 1984), 159-90. I had read it prior to going to India for the Kumbha Mela but I had forgotten it. I reread it after my return and gained much from it.

[2] Since then I have published three articles on the Kumbha Mela: M. Darrol Bryant, "A Kumbha Mela Notebook," *Dialogue and Alliance* 4.4 (1990-91): 86-100; "The Kumbha Mela As A Festival of Renewal," *Journal of Dharma*, 15.4, 341-56, and "River of Grace: The Kumbha Mela as a Sacred Place," *Environments*, 34-40. Some of the material included here has appeared in these earlier essays. For an important discussion of "field based" research—the basis of this paper—see T. N. Madan, "On Living Intimately With Strangers," in *Pathways: Approaches to the Study of Society in India* (New Delhi: Oxford University Press, 1994), 111-30.

[3] This is part of the title of the volume by Jack Hebner and David Osborn, *Kumbha Mela: The World's Largest Act of Faith,"* (LaJolla, CA: Entourage Publishing, 1990).

[4] For an interesting discussion of the pilgrim see the unpublished paper of Jana Duncan, "Kumbha Mela: The Changing Face of an Indian Pilgrimage," (Wilfrid Laurier University), 1999, available from M.D.Bryant. See also the wonderfully moving account of a pilgrimage to the sacred mountains of Wu T'ai in Northern China, its festivals, monasteries, and communities see John Blofeld, *The Wheel of Life*, (Boston: Shambhala, 1988), esp. 114-55. This account is even more precious given the destruction in the region after 1949. For a fascinating account of Rajasthani pilgrims, though not to the

Kumbha Mela, see Ann Grodzins Gold, *Fruitful Journeys, The Ways of Rajasthani Pilgrims* (Berkeley: University of California Press, 1988), which demonstrates the centrality of release or moksha to the pilgrims expectation and intention. Gold's study is a fine example of field research in which the scholar is aware of her own role in the study.

[5] The Hebner and Osborn volume, *Kumbha Mela*, is a visual feast, though it tends to focus on the exotic and the exceptional, as it contains some excellent pictures of the people and actions that happen at the Kumbha Mela.

[6] See the article byD. P. Dubey, "Kumbha Mela: Origin and Historicity of India's Greatest Pilgrimage Fair," and "Prayag and its Kumbha Mela," in *Kumbha Mela: Pilgrimage to the Greatest Cosmic Fair*, ed. D. P. Dubey (Allahbad: Society of Pilgrimage Studies, 2001), 85-123 and 1-49 respectively.

[7] One of the participants in an International Seminar on the Kumbha Mela held at the Kumbha Mela in 2001 spoke of these other "worldly" aspects of the Kumbha Mela, namely, its social and economic purposes.

[8] I have been trying to locate some of these sources in the sacred literature. I was told that you find these stories in the Bhagavad Purana, but while I found the story of the churning of the sea of milk and the producing of a pitcher of amrit, I could not find the story about its falling on the earth at Prayag. I would be grateful for your assistance in this. The things quoted here are from the Hari Krishna website on the Kumbha Mela 2001. The Bhagavad Purana is in volumes seven through eleven in the Ancient Indian Tradition and Mythology Series (Delhi: Motilal Banarsidass, 1987). The quotations here are from volume IX and indicate the book and verse. In the version, we find in the Bhagavad Purana, the churning of the oceans also brings forth a horse "radiantly white like the moon"(VIII.8.3) and an elephant with four tusks that "eclipsed the splendour and beauty of the snowy mountain, Kailasa"(VIII.8.4-6). But when the pitcher appeared, it created such a fuss, with everyone clambering for it, that, according to the Bhagavad Purana, it was seized by a divine messenger and returned to the heavens. However, before the Lord "flies away on Garuda"(VIII.10), Mohini, the Lord in a feminine form, is able to distribute, due to her beguiling ways, some of the nectar to the "gods" thus bestowing on them immortality (VIII.9).

Enroute we are told in other sources, and as battle erupts, some drops spilled on the earth and these sites became the places of the Festival.

[9] See Edwin Bernbaum, *Sacred Mountains of the World* (Berkeley: University of California Press, 1997).

[10] Mircea Eliade, *Patterns in Comparative Religion* (Cleveland: Meridian Books, 1963), 1ff.

[11] In 2001, Shrivatsa Goswami remarked that we could call the 2001 Kumbha Mela "the Festival of who has the loudest speaker system." I also noted that there were many more camps with neon lights at the entrance, there were the huge figures of Krishna and Caitanya at the Hari Krishna camp and a huge lighted pyramid at the north end of the site. There were also more parades during the 2001 Kumbha Mela and also more police. Shrivatsa said the extra security was due to "bomb threats that had been made against the Kumbha Mela."

[12] See the article on "Sacred Space" by Joel Brereton in the *Encyclopedia of Religion*, vol.12, ed., Mircea Eliade, (New York: Macmillan, 1987), 526ff.

[13] *Ibid.*

[14] These words are taken from my notebooks for January 24, 2001, at the Sri Caitanya Prema Samsthana Camp at the Kumbha Mela. That evening, Purushottam had agreed to discuss the Kumbha Mela with the people in the camp. He asked me to pose the questions. Shrivatsa Goswami translated from Hindi to English. I have given a copy of what I have reported here to Shrivatsa Goswami and he has confirmed their accuracy. The whole discourse went on for more than one hour.

[15] See the Bhavisyottara Purana 31,14.

[16] See Mircea Eliade, *Patterns of Comparative Religion*, 190, 194. See also other works by Mircea Eliade, *Myth and Reality* (New York: Harper & Row, 1963), esp. 39-54; *Man and the Sacred* (New York: Harper & Row, 1974), 77-115; and *Rites and Symbols of Initiation* (New York: Harper & Row, 1965).

About Pandora Press

Pandora Press is a small, independently owned press dedicated to making available modestly priced books that deal with Anabaptist, Mennonite, and Believers Church topics, both historical and theological. We welcome comments from our readers.

Visit our full-service online Bookstore:
www.pandorapress.com

Leah Dawn Bueckert and Daniel Schipani, eds. *Spiritual Caregiving in the Hospital. Windows to Chaplaincy Ministry* (Kitchener: Pandora Press, 2006) Softcover, 230 pages. ISBN 1-894710-65-7

Ralph Lebold, *Strange and Wonderful Paths. The Memoirs of Ralph Lebold.* (Kitchener: Pandora Press, 2006). Softcover, 236 pages. Bibliography, index. ISBN 1-894710-66-5

Karl Koop, ed. *Confessions of Faith in the Anabaptist Tradition, 1527-1660* ((Kitchener: Pandora Press, 2006). Softcover, 366 pages. Scripture index. ISBN 1-894710-62-2

Alle Hoekema and Hanspeter Jecker, eds. *Testing Faith and Tradition. A Global Mennonite History: Europe* (Kitchener: Pandora Press, 2006; co-published with Good Books) Softcover, 324 pages. Indexes. ISBN 1-56148-550-0

John A. Lapp and C. Arnold Snyder, gen.eds., *Anabaptist Songs in African Hearts. A Global Mennonite History: Africa* (Kitchener: Pandora Press, 2006; co-published with Good Books) Softcover, 292 pages. Indexes. ISBN 1-56148-549-7

Harry Loewen, *Between Worlds. Reflections of a Soviet-born Canadian Mennonite* (Kitchener: Pandora Press, 2006). Softcover, 358 pages. Bibliography. ISBN 1-894710-63-0

H. H. Drake Williams III, ed., *Caspar Schwenckfeld. Eight Writings on Christian Beliefs* (Kitchener: Pandora Press, 2006). Softcover, 200 pages. Index. ISBN 1-894710-64-9

Maureen Epp and Carol Ann Weaver, eds., *Sound in the Land: Essays on Mennonites and Music* (Kitchener: Pandora Press, 2006). Softcover, 220 pages. Bibliography. ISBN 1-894710-59-2

Geoffrey Dipple, *"Just as in the Time of the Apostles": Uses of History in the Radical Reformation* (Kitchener: Pandora Press, 2005). Softcover, 324 pages. Bibliography and index. ISBN 1-894710-58-4.

Harry Huebner, *Echoes of the Word: Theological Ethics as Rhetorical Practice* Anabaptist and Mennonite Studies Series (Kitchener: Pandora Press, 2005). Softcover, 274 pages. Bibliography and index. ISSN 1494-4081 ISBN 1-894710-56-8

John F. Haught, *Purpose, Evolution and the Mystery of Life,* Proceedings of the Fourth Annual Goshen Conference on Religion and Science, ed. Carl S. Helrich (Kitchener" Pandora Press, 2005). Softcover, 130 pages. Index. ISBN 1-894710-55-X

Gerald W. Schlabach, gen. ed., *Called Together to be Peacemakers: Report of the International Dialogue between the Catholic Church and Mennonite World Conference 1998-2003* (Kitchener: Pandora Press, 2005). Softcover, 77 pages. ISSN 1711-9480 ISBN 1-894710-57-6

Rodney James Sawatsky, *History and Ideology: American Mennonite Identity Definition through History* (Kitchener: Pandora Press, 2005). Softcover, 216 pages. Bibliography and index. ISBN 1-894710-53-3 ISSN 1494-4081

Harvey Neufeldt, Ruth Derksen Siemens and Robert Martens, eds., *First Nations and First Settlers in the Fraser Valley (1890-1960)* (Kitchener: Pandora Press, 2005). Softcover, 287 pages. Bibliography and index. ISBN 1-894710-54-1

David Waltner-Toews, *The Complete Tante Tina: Mennonite Blues and Recipes* (Kitchener: Pandora Press, 2004) Softcover, 129 pages. ISBN 1-894710-52-5

John Howard Yoder, *Anabaptism and Reformation in Switzerland: An Historical and Theological Analysis of the Dialogues Between Anabaptists and Reformers* (Kitchener: Pandora Press, 2004) Softcover, 509 pages. Bibliography and indexes. ISBN 1-894710-44-4 ISSN 1494-4081

Antje Jackelén, *The Dialogue Between Religion and Science: Challenges and Future Directions* (Kitchener: Pandora Press, 2004) Softcover, 143 pages. Index. ISBN 1-894710-45-2

Ivan J. Kauffman, ed., *Just Policing: Mennonite-Catholic Theological Colloquium 2001-2002* (Kitchener: Pandora Press, 2004). Softcover, 127 pages. ISBN 1-894710-48-7.

Gerald W. Schlabach, ed., *On Baptism: Mennonite-Catholic Theological Colloquium 2001-2002* (Kitchener: Pandora Press, 2004). Softcover, 147 pages., ISBN 1-894710-47-9 ISSN 1711-9480.

Harvey L. Dyck, John R. Staples and John B. Toews, comp., trans. and ed. *Nestor Makhno and the Eichenfeld Massacre:* (Kitchener: Pandora Press, 2004). Softcover, 115pages. ISBN 1-894710-46-0.

Jeffrey Wayne Taylor, *The Formation of the Primitive Baptist Movement* (Kitchener: Pandora Press, 2004). Softcover, 225 pages. Bibliography and index. ISBN 1-894710-42-8 ISSN 1480-7432.

James C. Juhnke and Carol M. Hunter, *The Missing Peace: The Search for Nonviolent Alternatives in United States History,* 2nd ed. (Kitchener: Pandora Press, 2004) Softcover, 339 pp. Index. ISBN 1-894710-46-3

Louise Hawkley and James C. Juhnke, eds., *Nonviolent America: History through the Eyes of Peace* (North Newton: Bethel College, 2004, co-published with Pandora Press) Softcover, 269 pages. Index. ISBN 1-889239-02-X

Karl Koop, *Anabaptist-Mennonite Confessions of Faith: the Development of a Tradition* (Kitchener: Pandora Press, 2004) Softcover, 178 pages. Index. ISBN 1-894710-32-0

Lucille Marr, *The Transforming Power of a Century: Mennonite Central Committee and its Evolution in Ontario* (Kitchener: Pandora Press, 2003). Softcover, 390 pages. Bibliography and index, ISBN 1-894710-41-x.

Erica Janzen, *Six Sugar Beets, Five Bitter Years* (Kitchener: Pandora Press, 2003). Softcover, 186 pages. ISBN 1-894710-37-1.

T. D. Regehr, *Faith Life and Witness in the Northwest, 1903–2003: Centenninal History of the Northwest Mennonite Conference* (Kitchener: Pandora Press, 2003). Softcover, 524 pages. Index, ISBN 1-894710-39-8.

George F. R. Ellis, *A Universe of Ethics Morality and Hope: Proceedings from the Second Annual Goshen Conference on Religion and Science* (Kitchener: Pandora Press, 2003) Softcover, 148 pages. ISBN 1-894710-36-3

Donald Martin, *Old Order Mennonites of Ontario: Gelassenheit, Discipleship, Brotherhood* (Kitchener: Pandora Press, 2003). Softcover, 381 pages. Index. ISBN 1-894710-33-9

Mary A. Schiedel, *Pioneers in Ministry: Women Pastors in Ontario Mennonite Churches, 1973-2003* (Kitchener: Pandora Press, 2003) Softcover, 204 pages. ISBN 1-894710-35-5

Harry Loewen, ed., *Shepherds, Servants and Prophets* (Kitchener: Pandora Press, 2003) Softcover, 446 pages. ISBN 1-894710-35-5

Robert A. Riall, trans., Galen A. Peters, ed., *The Earliest Hymns of the Ausbund: Some Beautiful Christian Songs Composed and Sung in the Prison at Passau, Published 1564* (Kitchener: Pandora Press, 2003) Softcover, 468 pages. Bibliography and index. ISBN 1-894710-34-7.

John A. Harder, *From Kleefeld With Love* (Kitchener: Pandora Press, 2003) Softcover, 198 pages. ISBN 1-894710-28-2

John F. Peters, *The Plain People: A Glimpse at Life Among the Old Order Mennonites of Ontario* (Kitchener: Pandora Press, 2003) Softcover, 54 pages. ISBN 1-894710-26-6

Robert S. Kreider, *My Early Years: An Autobiography* (Kitchener: Pandora Press, 2002) Softcover, 600 pages. Index ISBN 1-894710-23-1

Helen Martens, *Hutterite Songs* (Kitchener: Pandora Press, 2002) Softcover, xxii, 328 pages. ISBN 1-894710-24-X

C. Arnold Snyder and Galen A. Peters, eds., *Reading the Anabaptist Bible: Reflections for Every Day of the Year* (Kitchener: Pandora Press, 2002) Softcover, 415 pages. ISBN 1-894710-25-8

C. Arnold Snyder, ed., *Commoners and Community: Essays in Honour of Werner O. Packull* (Kitchener: Pandora Press, 2002) Softcover, 324 pages. ISBN 1-894710-27-4

James O. Lehman, *Mennonite Tent Revivals: Howard Hammer and Myron Augsburger, 1952-1962* (Kitchener: Pandora Press, 2002) Softcover, xxiv, 318 pages. ISBN 1-894710-22-3

Lawrence Klippenstein and Jacob Dick, *Mennonite Alternative Service in Russia* (Kitchener: Pandora Press, 2002) Softcover, viii, 163 pages. ISBN 1-894710-21-5

Nancey Murphy, *Religion and Science* (Kitchener: Pandora Press, 2002) Softcover, 126 pages. ISBN 1-894710-20-7

Biblical Concordance of the Swiss Brethren, 1540. Trans. Gilbert Fast and Galen Peters; bib. intro. Joe Springer; ed. C. Arnold Snyder (Kitchener: Pandora Press, 2001) Softcover, lv, 227 pages. ISBN 1-894710-16-9

Orland Gingerich, *The Amish of Canada* (Kitchener: Pandora Press, 2001) Softcover, 244 pages. Index. ISBN 1-894710-19-3

M. Darrol Bryant, *Religion in a New Key* (Kitchener: Pandora Press, 2001) Softcover, 136 pages. Bib. refs. ISBN 1-894710- 18-5

Trans. Walter Klaassen, Frank Friesen, Werner O. Packull, ed. C. Arnold Snyder, *Sources of South German/Austrian Anabaptism* (Kitchener: Pandora Press, 2001; co-published with Herald Press.) Softcover, 430 pages. Indexes. ISBN 1-894710-15-0

Pedro A. Sandín Fremaint y Pablo A. Jimémez, *Palabras Duras: Homilías* (Kitchener: Pandora Press, 2001). Softcover, 121 pages. ISBN 1-894710-17-7

Ruth Elizabeth Mooney, *Manual Para Crear Materiales de Educación Cristiana* (Kitchener: Pandora Press, 2001). Softcover, 206 pages. ISBN 1-894710-12-6

Esther and Malcolm Wenger, poetry by Ann Wenger, *Healing the Wounds* (Kitchener: Pandora Press, 2001). Softcover, 210 pages. ISBN 1-894710-09-6.

Otto H. Selles and Geraldine Selles-Ysselstein, *New Songs* (Kitchener: Pandora Press, 2001). Poetry and relief prints, 90 pages. ISBN 1-894719-14-2

Pedro A. Sandín Fremaint, *Cuentos y Encuentros: Hacia una Educación Transformadora* (Kitchener: Pandora Press, 2001). Softcover 163 pages. ISBN 1-894710-08-8.

A. James Reimer, *Mennonites and Classical Theology: Dogmatic Foundations for Christian Ethics* (Kitchener: Pandora Press, 2001) Softcover, 650pages. ISBN 0-9685543-7-7

Walter Klaassen, *Anabaptism: Neither Catholic nor Protestant*, 3rd ed (Kitchener: Pandora Press, 2001) Softcover, 122pages. ISBN 1-894710-01-0

Dale Schrag & James Juhnke, eds., *Anabaptist Visions for the new Millennium: A search for identity* (Kitchener: Pandora Press, 2000) Softcover, 242 pages. ISBN 1-894710-00-2

Harry Loewen, ed., *Road to Freedom: Mennonites Escape the Land of Suffering* (Kitchener: Pandora Press, 2000) Hardcover, large format, 302pages. ISBN 0-9685543-5-0

Alan Kreider and Stuart Murray, eds., *Coming Home: Stories of Anabaptists in Britain and Ireland* (Kitchener: Pandora Press, 2000) Softcover, 220pages. ISBN 0-9685543-6-9

Edna Schroeder Thiessen and Angela Showalter, *A Life Displaced: A Mennonite Woman's Flight from War-Torn Poland* (Kitchener: Pandora Press, 2000) Softcover, xii, 218pages. ISBN 0-9685543-2-6

Stuart Murray, *Biblical Interpretation in the Anabaptist Tradition*, Studies in the Believers Tradition (Kitchener: Pandora Press, 2000) Softcover, 310pages. ISBN 0-9685543-3-4 ISSN 1480-7432.

Loren L. Johns, ed. *Apocalypticism and Millennialism* (Kitchener: Pandora Press, 2000) Softcover, 419pages. Indexes. ISBN 0-9683462-9-4 ISSN 1480-7432

Later Writings by Pilgram Marpeck and his Circle. Volume 1. Trans. Walter Klaassen, Werner Packull, and John Rempel (Kitchener: Pandora Press, 1999) Softcover, 157pages. ISBN 0-9683462-6-X

John Driver, *Radical Faith. An Alternative History of the Christian Church,* ed. Carrie Snyder. Kitchener: Pandora Press, 1999) Softcover, 334pages. ISBN 0-9683462-8-6

C. Arnold Snyder, *From Anabaptist Seed.* (Kitchener: Pandora Press, 1999) Softcover, 53pages. ISBN 0-9685543-0-X
   Also available in Spanish translation: *De Semilla Anabautista,* from Pandora Press only.

John D. Thiesen, *Mennonite and Nazi? Attitudes Among Mennonite Colonists in Latin America, 1933-1945* (Kitchener: Pandora Press, 1999) Softcover, 330pages. Bibliography, index. ISBN 0-9683462-5-1

Lifting the Veil, ed. Leonard Friesen; trans. Walter Klaassen (Kitchener: Pandora Press, 1998). Softcover, 128pages. ISBN 0-9683462-1-9

Leonard Gross, *The Golden Years of the Hutterites,* rev. ed. (Kitchener: Pandora Press, 1998). Softcover, 280pages. Index. ISBN 0-9683462-3-5

William H. Brackney, ed., *The Believers Church: A Voluntary Church,* (Kitchener: Pandora Press, 1998). Softcover, viii, 237pages. Index. ISBN 0-9683462-0-0 ISSN 1480-7432.

An Annotated Hutterite Bibliography, compiled by Maria H. Krisztinkovich, ed. by Peter C. Erb (Kitchener: Pandora Press, 1998). (Ca. 2,700 entries) 312pages., softcover, electronic, or both. ISBN (paper) 0-9698762-8-9/(disk) 0-9698762-9-7

Jacobus ten Doornkaat Koolman, *Dirk Philips. Friend and Colleague of Menno Simons,* trans. W. E. Keeney, ed. C. A. Snyder (Kitchener: Pandora Press, 1998). Softcover, xviii, 236pages. Index. ISBN: 0-9698762-3-8

Sarah Dyck, ed./tr., *The Silence Echoes: Memoirs of Trauma & Tears* (Kitchener: Pandora Press, 1997). Softcover, xii, 236pages. ISBN: 0-9698762-7-0

Wes Harrison, *Andreas Ehrenpreis and Hutterite Faith and Practice* (Kitchener: Pandora Press, 1997). Softcover, xxiv, 274pages. Index. ISBN 0-9698762-6-2

C. Arnold Snyder, *Anabaptist History and Theology: Revised Student Edition* (Kitchener: Pandora Press, 1997). Softcover, xiv, 466pages. Index, bibliography. ISBN 0-9698762-5-4

Nancey Murphy, *Reconciling Theology and Science: A Radical Reformation Perspective* (Kitchener, Ont.: Pandora Press, 1997). Softcover, x, 103pages. Index. ISBN 0-9698762-4-6

The Limits of Perfection: A Conversation with J. Lawrence Burkholder 2nd ed., with a new epilogue by J. Lawrence Burkholder, Rodney Sawatsky and Scott Holland, eds. (Kitchener: Pandora Press, 1996). Softcover, x, 154pages. ISBN 0-9698762-2-X

C. Arnold Snyder, *Anabaptist History and Theology: An Introduction* (Kitchener: Pandora Press, 1995). ISBN 0-9698762-0-3 Softcover, x, 434pages. Index,bibliography.

Pandora Press
33 Kent Avenue Kitchener, ON N2G 3R2

Tel.: (519) 578-2381 / Fax: (519) 578-1826
E-mail: info@pandorapress.com
Web site: www.pandorapress.com